Rohit-Man of Master Class 2.0

LAL AND SONS PRODUCTIONS PVT LTD

PRESENTS

Abhinav Lall

ISBN: 978-93-87852-45-7

First Published: August 2018

Cover Design
Swarnava Bera

Distributed by

shopcluse.com
power-publishers.com
readwhere.com
infibeam.com
snapdeal.com
flipkart.com
amazon.com
amazon.in
ebay.in

2nd of November, 2013. The crowd of MA.Chinnaswamy, Bangalore was all set for the 7th ODI between India and Australia. After winning the toss, India was put on to bat by the Kangaroos. There was some special atmosphere set by one of the Indian openers out there and the 30000 people crowd was a witness of it.

Final over of the Indian innings, 197*, three runs short of creating history. McKay starts with his run-up, finger pumped over the bowl. Batsman, in a tensed situation and wondering to make this ball a memorable one. The crowd begins to chant his name. McKay bowls it full outside off. He plays a lofted inside out drive over extra covers for a six.

"He goes inside out and what a way to bring up 200 in One Day Internationals. They call him HITMAN and he is arrived into the party.

An outstanding double hundred (200) for.............." – Ravi Shashtri commented.

Vote of Thanks

We would like to thank all individuals as well as the team who took part in this wonderful project and contributed in the best way they can.

First of all we would like to thank none other than but MR. Rohit Sharma, the person on whom this book has been published.

Secondly we would like to thank MR. Aneesh Gautam who precisely helped us with all the intellectuals and proceedings.

Our sincere thanks to 'ROURKELA SPORTS ASSOCIATION' and MR. Mihir Ray (Secretary) for being a wonderful organiser for the launching ceremony.

A huge thanks to each and everyone who helped and gave us the platform for the promotional events all throught out the city.

We would also like to thank our Associated Parter, Media Partner, Social Partner, Publishing Partner and Distributers all over.

INTRODUCTION

The time which is going through means to be the time of complete sports revolution. That revolution includes everything, cricket as well. Cricket has been the most crazy thing for the peoples of the world to enjoy. Almost 39% of the world's population is connected to the game either directly or indirectly. This particular book describes the same religion known as cricket but in a personal and depicted manner. This is a biography of none other than but India's most talented and high rated star "ROHIT GURUNATH SHARMA"

Every country has craze for this man but obviously the Indian people love him the most out of anyone else. The kind of image and reputation he has set out there between the 22 yards in the spherical ground is absolutely remarkable. There are many cricketers in India who are above par Rohit Sharma but every Gem has its own quality and features. Similarly when the reader will come across this biography he will find that the journey of HITMAN is divided in three major categories which is described later in the book.

Rohit Sharma has millions and billions of fans throughout the world. At this course of time, the kind of momentum he is in and the sort of confidence he possess is just enough to cross every big cricketer in today's era.

The biography not only is interesting and a complete story teller about Rohit but also it will work as an inspiration for each and everyone who will read the book. No matter what age, sex or anything, the type of contents the book has, it would change the mindset of many people in the world.

The people who think life will give them a opportunity but after reading this biography they will know that life doesn't give any opportunity rather you have to compel life to give a small thread which later on you can turn it as a rope. Just similarly how Rohit did it.

The aim and motive of this biography is to inspire everyone especially the youngsters out there. When these youngsters will get across the struggle and success of Rohit Sharma, they will not run away or deny to struggle in their life but they will like to enjoy that. The biography also tells peoples many facts and incidents related to Rohit Sharma.

Acknowledgement

The complete process of this book right from the beginning till the end wouldn't have been successful without the influence of these many personalities. They all contributed in my ambition to write this biography directly or indirectly, financially or advisedly. The most important contribution is that of my father from anyone else Mr. Pankaj Kumar Lall, who sacrificed a lot for this dream. I would also like to thank my whole family and management for believing in me and appreciating me for my good deeds.

And finally I would like to thank all the inferior personalities who gave me all the informations, guidance, advises and support to make this project a successful one. It wouldn't have been possible without you all. ☺

Major contributions:-

MR. P.K LALL (father), MRS.NEETA LALL (mother), ROHIT SHARMA (admirer), POWER PUBLISHERS, very importantly MR. ANEESH GAUTAM and the complete family who is connected to entitle "LAL". It would not have been possible without you all guys.

DISCLAIMER

The intention of the book is to inspire as many people it can and tell the world about the complete ongoing life of one of world's finest cricketer ROHIT SHARMA. It does not aim to hurt anyone personal feelings, beliefs, etc. The book doesn't provide any fake news or facts about the cricketer and doesn't support any situations related to it. The biography has been written in a simple English language keeping in mind that every person from various age, various background and various skills can read the book and understand the story.

Please note:- As Rohit Sharma is currently playing, this book describes Rohit only till the IPL 2018. All the stats and records took under consideration are within this time period.

Contents

1. BIRTH AND SLOW ATTENTION FOR CRICKET: -

Every family dreams to have a child who can later on take their name to the level high. Similarly one of the normal middle class family known as Sharma's dreamt of the same thing and if we see that situation today we will say they were not at all disappointed with the dream they saw. On 30th of April, 1987 (Thursday), at Nagpur, Maharashtra, India, god blessed them with a child who was completely filled with talent within himself. All the family members were quite happy to have him. He was none other than 'ROHIT SHARMA".

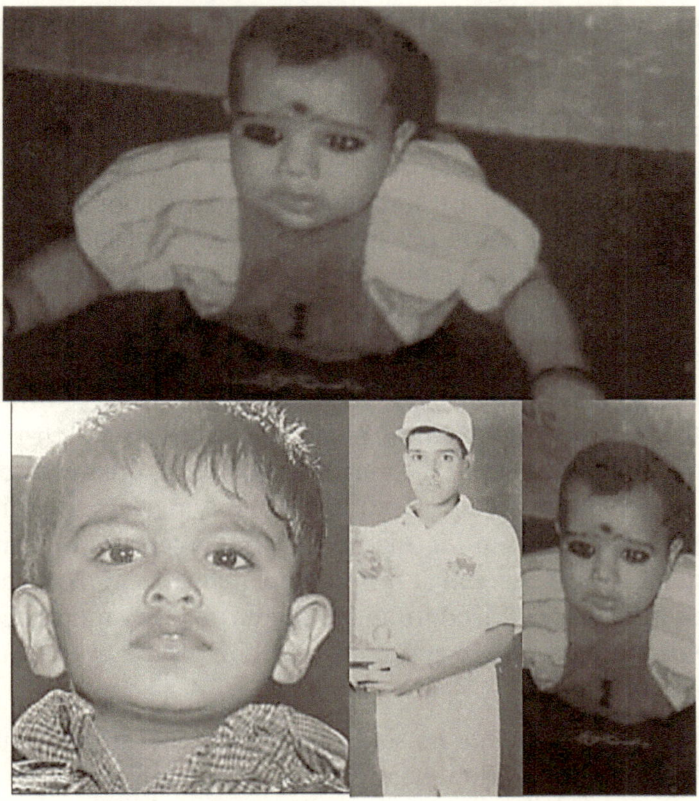

Every parent expects something from their young ones. When Rohit took birth its quite obvious that his parents must have dreamt as well that some or the other day he will make them proud with their head held high. But to be honest no one would have imagined that this fellow will do that to this level. Born with so much of talent and capability which later on came to be his finest quality and strength. Though Rohit doesn't like when he gets identified by the word 'talent' and rightly so because he believes its not his talent which have brought him under the umbrella of success but it's definitely his hard work and dedication towards the game. As he started his career as an off spin bowler and later on worked hard to achieve batting skills, he believes nothing came naturally to him rather he worked hard onto it. But the normal people including me watch him as their own point of view and firmly believes that he is completely filled with talent. Being a boy its quite impossible and extra ordinary if he doesn't move his steps towards cricket. Towards cricket doesn't means straight away playing it rather watching it and talking about it. Like how everything starts on an indirect way and later on it brings you on a direct note, similarly like that. Rohit started following cricket at a very young age and soon got motivated towards the game and fell in love with it.

Rohit was now just eleven years old when his love affair with the game stood up at point. He loved to watch the game and observed all the players closely. He dreamt to be there one day where he used to see many players. Slowly he became the fan of many Indian players who were genuinely professional at this game. Sachin Tendulkar and Virender Sehwag used to be his favourite. This motivated Rohit more and more and reminded him all the time what he wanted to be.

He has achievements not only on the cricket ground but right at the police stations as well as the people of his own locality filed a FIR against him. They were ultimately fed-up by this fellow and his cricket as not a single window was left on to be crashed by Master Rohit Sharma. After the normal threatening of the police uncles, Rohit unwillingly, stopped to showcase his talent in the society. When Rohit was in sixth (6th) standard, he joined a local club during his summer holidays. He rather joined the club as an off-spinner than a proper batsman due to the reason that there were already too many batters and the team were looking for a bowling all rounder who can bat a bit. And he wanted to get into the team any how so he used to act and play as a proper bowler. He started batting lower down the order at no.8 or no.9 as a tail-ender. When Rohit was in 7th standard, he thought of becoming a professional cricketer.

While going to his coaching ground which was situated at Church gate, he used to travel in a local train from Borivalli. Once while travelling to the ground as we all know about the condition of Mumbai local, Rohit anyway managed to get into it, but on the way due to so much of crowd his balance over his kit bag which had wheels of its own dropped out from the train compartment. Then Rohit after getting down into the next station went back to that spot but there was nothing found. Due to this incident, he was late to reach the ground and his coach didn't allowed him to bat that day as a punishment and Rohit was just asked to field. In an U-12 tournament at 1999, going through that he had to perform to be in the team. So, being nervous and tensed out there in the middle he had to deliver with whatever he is asked to do. Handed over the bowl, Rohit must be thinking in couple of aspects. First, being confident that yes why not... I can do it, I have the capacity to deliver. Secondly, if I don't deliver now I may get dropped or shattered from the team. Well this thing happens with all of us. Despite being under pressure, he holded his nerves quite well as he took couple of crucial wickets for the team which brought him infront of everyone's eyes and more importantly made him a winner under his own complexion.

Suddenly in a local match, Rohit was batting beautifully despite of coming lower down the order as a tail ender. He was not perfectly timing the ball but was going hard onto the bowlers smashing them all over the park. During this innings, his coach, Dinesh Lad, found something special in that young child. Even previously also some of his furious innings at the end impressed his coach. He asked Rohit to attend the nets session and allowed him to bat there. Watching him bat, his coach exceptionally felt that there is something within the child which can be really worth attaining if handled with care. Soon his coach decided to promote Rohit up the order and asked him to open the innings in the "Giles Shield Tournament" match. While moving his feets simultaneously in the ground, he could definitely fell some extra pressure as he was handed with a lot more responsibility and as he was getting close to that 22 yards pitch, the butterflies in his stomach were getting multiplied. The boy provided with an opportunity to prove his capability with the wooden willow in his hands didn't disappoint as he scored a mind blowing 140 odd runs under a lot more pressure than previous situations in that match. He attracted every single person and his attention towards himself as he played some magnificent and extra ordinary shots. This performance from him gave him the confidence and statement about himself. That particular innings changed his point of view towards the game. He realised that he had to work hard and harder until he attains some thing in this field. Then onwards he started to play as a proper all rounder, wherever he played.

And hence, the journey of a flawless magnificent player named 'ROHIT SHARMA' was on the runway and completely ready to take off.

2. EARLY LIFE AND FAMILY

Rohit Sharma in his early life has seen the worst of situations in all departments whether it is financially, physically or mentally. His father, Gurunath Sharma was a caretaker in some transport firm and his mom, Purnima Sharma was a housewife. Rohit's family were all cricket lovers. Almost everyone in his family have played some cricket not professionally but practically for schools and colleges. His dad was a very much fan of Test Cricket because he used to believe that its the only format of the game where everything is tested. Character, temperament, mind set, skills, patience, etc etc. This is the reason why Rohit wants to do well in test cricket to make his father happy.

Coming back to early life, initially he used to live with his family in Dombivalli, east Mumbai. But due to his father's low income, the situation was so much worse that they were unable to take proper care of him as well. So finally Rohit's parents decided to send him to his uncle's and grandparent's house which was situated at Borivalli. Rohit now started living with them. He would visit his parents to meet only at weekends. He later on changed his school and moved to Swami Vivekanand International School as it had better cricketing facilities, on recommendation of his cricket coach so that it could help him in his cricketing path. Hearing this news, Rohit's father and uncle felt really good to see young Rohit getting good platforms. Though Rohit felt really troubled to change it because he didn't wanted to get separated from his friends and colleagues. But this move was career changing one for Rohit.

Rohit told his coach that he couldn't afford it but his coach being aware of his talent and class got him a scholarship, so for four long years, Rohit was able to take all the benefits without even paying a penny. His coach, Dinesh Lad says, **"If that scholarship wouldn't have sanctioned, Indian Cricket may not be having Rohit Sharma today."** He did very well in cricket there. Rohit convinced his uncle, Ravi Sharma to give Rs. 200 to attend the coaching camp conducted by his coach. He has a younger brother, Vishal Sharma who is a very genuine person. After the discussion among Rohit's parents and his grandparents, it was decided that one of the two brothers would live with them and the other one would be living with their grandparents. So, it was decided that Rohit shall be living with their grandparents and Vishal will have to live with his parents. Both used to co-operate with each other and had shared a good bond among themselves.

Its quite important for a child to see tough days and situations though their parents would never like to show their kids such circumstances. But these are the only conditions which inspire a child to do something in their life, just like what happened with Rohit Sharma. All the worst situations motivated him to do well in life in any field so that his own kids could not face this trouble someday.

Rohit choosed his cricketing career before anything else and he completely dominated it. The struggle and problems

Rohit faced were immense but the young child was not worried of all this. His family members backed him and supported him and his dreams in whatever he wanted to be. The family support is one of the most important things for success. Initially Rohit and his family could barely afford to eat. These are the days only that contributed to make Rohit Sharma, a Ro-Super hit Sharma.

3. ROHIT'S INSPIRATION

Everyone in this world needs to get motivated and inspired watching someone from the similar field as they are. Whatever the job is, there is always an inspiration that inspires you to do it in a best way. Its not easy though. Many peoples first get inspired and then later on starts to do what their role model does in a typical manner. Similar theory is applicable in sports as well. Young kids when watch the legends of the game normally either live or with the help of any medium, they get inspired and that particular person becomes his/her role model.

In relation to cricket, kids who were born in the 90's era, 93% of them had their idol as Sachin Tendulkar. That particular era was completely dominated by that man. People believed him as a God who is disguised as a human. Rohit Sharma who was born in the same phase watched Sachin many a times and soon Rohit's mind and thinking was annexed by him. He started to follow Sachin. Whatever Sachin did, this fellow followed. Slowly and firmly the time came when Rohit saw him as his idol and role model. He also dreamt to play and share dressing room with Sachin one day.

Rohit was inspired by Sachin due to many reasons. Mainly his hard work, determination and dedication towards the game, passion for cricket. Not only this but both of them came from the same locality as the two were mumbaikars and their early life story was quite similar to each other as well. Rohit followed Sachin's path in every possible way he can. Initially Sachin also used to live with his sister and not with his parents and the same course of wind passes across Rohit's story too.

Rohit admits:-

"The kind of stuff he (Sachin) did when he was young to exactly where he is right now, I think he is a perfect role model for every youngster in our country. That's one of the reasons why I follow his cricket and footsteps."

Rohit has followed another player very closely who must be his second idol after Sachin. He (idol) too is a legend within himself. Rohit wanted to be the explosion like Virender Sehwag. He also wanted to have such fire and hitting power inside him. Rohit loved Viru very much mainly his attacking game. Once Rohit bunked his school to watch Viru bat. This shows his determination and passion for cricket. Besides them, Rohit also loved Ricky Ponting.

Very intelligent persons have said that to achieve your dream first you have to see it and its not what you see during sleep its the thing that doesn't let you sleep. Rohit dreamed to be like Sachin and Sehwag which is the main reason of his success today.

When during a function Sachin was asked that, **"who do you think can break your records??"**

He stood up from the chair, turned around and replied:-

"I think they are sitting in this room only. That bunch of youngsters.......

I think Virat and ROHIT are the ones who can do this."

Sachin further adds:

"Till the time if an Indian beats it, I don't have any problem. Records are made to be broken." ☺

Rohit's statement on his inspiration, Sachin Tendulkar:-

"When I (Rohit) came here in the team, I watched him (Sachin) from close quarters and I have seen how he works, how he operates in his day to day life, whether it is on the field or off the field. Its something very encouraging for any youngster."

Rohit further adds:-

"His humility and his simplicity was something which really took me by surprise. I have always looked up to him for advice, to show us the way and Sachin Paaji has really helped not just me but all the youngsters in the team. He has shown us the way which he has been doing through his career.

That's how it is, that's how the great legends are and he is one of them."

When Rohit was asked in a promotional event that what's the biggest motivation he carries through??

He proudly replies: **"well playing for my country is my biggest motivation."**

He further adds: **"once you wear the Indian jersey, it is motivation enough to go and perform on the field. If you are not motivated enough wearing the blue one, then you are just doing yourself a favour by showing up to the ground."**

-Rohit Sharma-

4. ENTRY TO NATIONAL AND DOMESTIC CRICKET.

After Rohit Sharma's hardwork and dedication, many cricket experts found that he is now very well prepared to enter cricket which now was known as professional level. Rohit was very well prepared after being a consistent performer in his local, school and club matches. He impressed his coach and many more through his cricketing mind and abilities.

At the age of 18, Rohit made his List A debut for west zone against central zone in the Deodhar Trophy in march 2005. He was all set at Gwalior for his debut. Rohit should be in a confident mind, happy to got an opportunity to deliver. Though confident, he must be a bit over tensed as well and its a very obvious thing making debut at a level after which people will treat you as a professional player is not that easy. There is humungous difference between school cricket and List or First Class Cricket. Rohit, initially could not deliver in the way he would have wanted and was getting out early in his innings. But all days are not the same. In the same tournament, against North Zone, Rohit got to a brilliant hundred taking his personal score to 142 runs off just 123 balls at Udaipur. This particular innings of Rohit brought him into the limelight. Rohit was now a well experienced and reputed player at these levels.

Before being selected in the Ranji team, Rohit performed well for India A side in Abu Dhabi and then followed by Australia. Looking at these consistent performances of Rohit, selectors selected him for the probable 30 members squad for Champions Trophy. Though he was not joined in the final squad but the youngster had many things to achieve in the upcoming years.

Rohit made his First Class debut against New Zealand A at Darwin in July 2006. Followed by another debut made for his Ranji team, Mumbai, in the 2006/07 season. Rohit went to a slow start as he didn't make out in the initial games but this boy never thought of giving up and was thrill to beats. In the match against Gujarat, Rohit moved on to score a mammal double hundred finishing up with 205 off 267. This innings provided more confidence to the mumbaikar which was beneficial for his team as well. Mumbai was into the finals and there too when team required of a good innings by someone, Rohit stood up and contributed with his half century in tough situation against Bengal. Later, Mumbai went on to win the tournament.

Here are the stats of Rohit Sharma's First Class Career:-

Matches:- 85

Runs:- 6456

Batting Avg :- 54.71

100/50:- 20/29

Best Score:- 309*

Balls Bowled:- 2,104

Wickets:- 24

Best Figures:- 4 for 41

Catches:- 66

The win in the Ranji Trophy led to U-19 debut for Rohit Sharma. Due to his good performance in FC cricket, he was selected for the upcoming U-19 world cup for the team in 2006. He performed quite well over there. He ended with the third highest run getter for India in that tournament. Though India went to the finals, they couldn't win it. But all the experts were alarmed about the upcoming talent in the Indian team, Rohit Sharma.

Rohit's stats in U-19 CWC 2006:-

Matches:- 6

Innings:- 6

Runs:- 205

Not Out:- 1

Best Score:- 78

Average:- 41.00

Balls Faced:- 265

Strike Rate:- 77.35

100/50:- 0/3

4's/6's:- 18/4

5. LOVE AND PASSION TOWARDS THE GAME

All of us needs to be enough passionate to do something in our life. Without passion and dedication nothing can be achieved. And when this application is applied on the sports category, its meaning is thoroughly practicalised. To play any sport in the best way, correct dedication and love is very much necessary to do well. These are the qualities which are performed initially in the ages and later on by the further course of time starts disappearing which sometimes stand as the main reason behind failures.

Rohit Sharma, enough dedicated, passionate and full of charge had all the qualities which a cricketer needs to achieve fame. His love towards the game is just beyond par. Whether it may be few decades back or today, the passion of Rohit to play cricket is the same. The graph once started to raise few years back never fell down and kept on achieving more elevation. It just only increased day by day and match by match. And when it comes to cricket, its not an easy work to have the same dedication right from start till you face the last ball of your career.

Rohit believes that whatever a person does, he needs to give his 100% and commit to it fully just exactly he (Rohit) did it to pursue his dreams.

During an event at SNBP School, Rohit states, **"I always had that will that no matter what I will always give my best in whatever I am doing whether its studies or cricket. And thats what I did, I committed to it fully and yes my dreams are not over yet. I still want more so I am looking forward to it".**

These statements made by Rohit clarifies the screen about how much he was connected to his game and what all he had done to live up his dreams. Sacrifices, hard work, determination are the activities which he performed to get on to the top today. Without attraction for cricket, he couldn't have done these activities and without these activities, cricket may not have got this superstar. Cricket has always been Rohit's priority. Whatever dream he lives today is of his own and also because of his love and passion that he carries for cricket and may carry long and very long.

6. JOURNEY AND INTERACTION WITH THE IPL

Indian Premier League (IPL). Well it won't be unfair to say that IPL has been the most successful domestic tournament in the world in the one last decade. It all started when the game of cricket was getting shorter and shorter and thus the shortest format of the game was first introduced in 2007 as World T20. After observing the brand new format and its success all over the world, Board of Cricket Control in India (BCCI) decided to bring up the same format here as well to create opportunities for the youngsters of India.

Rohit Sharma, in present time, is one of the finest player in the league. Due to his good display of talent at the World T20, it gave him the opportunity to appear in the IPL. He was signed up by one of the franchise 'Deccan Chargers' for a sum of US \$ 750,000 in 2008. He was one of the leading run scorer in that season and held the orange cup for a brief period too. In the next season, Rohit was declared as the vice captain of the team. On 6th may 2009, we can say that Rohit's first major achievement came through and crashed with him. Mumbai Indians, the opposition. Deccan Chargers, batting first managed to score 145 runs with Rohit being the architect of the batting line up, scoring 38 runs. No need to worry the achievement I am talking about is something else which even Rohit wouldn't have expected. The match seemed to be balanced pretty well. Mumbai was very comfortable as JP Duminy was there in the middle. Asking 46 runs in the last 5 over wasn't a sweaty task. Then Mr. Gilly plays a gamble by giving Rohit-the part timer, 16th over of the match. He conceded 3 runs in his first 4 deliveries. Fifth ball............ bowled!!

Full and angled towards the leg stump of Abhishek Nayar and he attempts for a paddle sweep unfortunately missing it completely to get bowled out. First one down!

Next comes Harbhajan Singh and his attempt to clear the mid wicket fence shatters as bhajji departs with a golden duck as his inside edge crashed the stumps. Rohit gets two-in-two!!

The 18th over begins, Sharma ready to bowl his hat-trick delivery inducing a thick edge from Duminy's bat which was very well caught by Gilchrist behind the stumps. An unexpected hat-trick for Rohit Sharma. Chargers went onto win the game by 19 runs and ended the league lifting the cup.

We would say the first few seasons just began the journey of Hitman but the turning point came when he was picked by another franchise, 'Mumbai Indians' for US $ 2 million in 2011. This team came up as a lucky charm for Rohit. He scored his debut ton in the IPL against Kolkata Knight Riders (KKR) ending with 109* off 60 balls at Eden Gardens.

Rohit Sharma from 2008 to 2012 in IPL

(5 seasons)

<u>2008</u>

Team: Deccan Chargers

Matches: 13

Runs: 404

Average: 36.72

Strike Rate: 147.98

Best score: 76*

100/50: 0/4

4’s/6’s: 38/19

2009

Team: Deccan Chargers

Matches: 16

Runs: 362

Average: 27.84

Strike Rate: 114.92

Best score: 52

100/50: 0/1

4’s/6’s: 22/18

Bowling:-

Matches: 16

Balls: 138

Runs conceded: 161

Wickets: 11 (1 hat trick)

Best figures: 4/6

Average: 14.63

Economy: 7.00

2010

Team: Deccan Chargers

Matches: 16

Runs: 404

Average: 28.85

Strike Rate: 133.77

Best score: 73

100/50: 0/3

4's/6's: 36/14

<u>2011</u>

Team: Mumbai Indians

Matches: 16

Runs: 372

Average: 33.81

Strike Rate: 125.25

Best score: 87

100/50: 0/3

4's/6's: 32/13

<u>2012</u>

Team: Mumbai Indians

Matches: 17

Runs: 433

Average: 30.92

Strike Rate: 126.60

Best score: 109*

100/50: 1/3

4's/6's: 39/18

Season 6 (2013):-

Under the captaincy of Ricky Ponting, MI started their 6th edition of the IPL. Though the start was not up to the mark and what we fans expected, the franchise could see still a ray of hope. After loosing the game against RCB (Royal Challengers Bangalore), Mumbai managed to win their next game against DD (Delhi Daredevils). The openers were once again sent back at cheap scores throwing Mumbai in a shrinking position. It was the efforts of Dinesh Karthik and Rohit Sharma that took MI to a formidable score of 209. This effort led to the victory of 44 runs. A couple of games later against RR (Rajasthan Royals), Indians were buckled up for just 92 runs and due to this out-dated performance, Ricky Ponting stepped down from captaincy and retired from all forms of the game. It was now our HITMAN who took the campaign of "Duniya hila denge hum" upon his shoulders. Under his captaincy, MI recovered from their initial shocks and went on to become the 'CHAMPIONS' for the very first time beating CSK (Chennai Super Kings) in the finals.

Rohit in IPL 2013:-

Team: Mumbai Indians

Matches: 19

Runs: 538

Average: 38.42

Strike Rate: 131.54

Best score: 79*

100/50: 0/4

4's/6's: 35/28

The winning chariot of Mumbai did not took a halt here itself as the year 2013 had other plans for the team. The team carried the same momentum they took from IPL in the Champions League Twenty-20 too. The leader was none other than Rohit- 'The Great Sharma'. The initial stage of the tournament was quite similar to the particular year's IPL. But 'slow and steady wins the race' is the quote that MI lives upon. They know the art of comeback drastically well. They won the do or die game against Perth Scorchers which was their last league match under the efforts of Rohit, Dwayne Smith and Coulter-Nile. In the finals, the IPL champions posted a mammal 202 runs on the board which later on resulted in a 33 runs victory. After this win, the small captaincy career of Rohit gave him many to remember. He now had couple of huge trophies under his belt.

Season 7 (2014):-

Rohit had already compelled people to accept that his batting skills and standard are just beyond good but now whatever happened was turning litmus blue in the field of leadership and its skills. Rohit was examined many a times but he was completely ready to play a new role as a captain and he not only to grabbed it with both the hands but also gave some cut off answers to some tough situations.

In the 7th edition of the Indian Premier League, MI loosed all the 5 games they played in UAE (United Arab Emirates) but the skipper surely manufactures some confidence capsules and provides to his team. He was pretty sure that the team has the capability to turn the tables around very oftenly what they did last year. Rohit says:-

"We all know its a disappointing start, we committed too many mistakes and kept repeating them. Well that can happen... its a new team but its a difficult challenge now. We are back to our home ground and crowd. We would like to do the same as we did last year. I hope we won't commit the mistakes we did and if we keep doing the right things, I am sure thing will fall in place."

This statement made by Rohit shows he had that attitude and mindset what a successful skipper requires. Though MI did not went on to win that season as the mighty CSK (Chennai Super Kings) defeated the defending champions in the eliminator but sometimes its not the win that decorates you character but its obviously your fighting attitude that does.

Rohit in IPL 2014:-

Team: Mumbai Indians

Matches: 15

Runs: 390

Average: 30.00

Strike Rate: 129.13

Best score: 59*

100/50: 0/3

4's/6's: 31/16

Season 8 (2015):-

Rohit and company came back strongly the very next season. But the slow starters again started slowly with 4 initial defeats. Though Rohit personally took off to a flier scoring 98* against KKR (Kolkata Knight Riders) in the first game of the tournament. But Rohit believed in his team's success than achieving his personal milestones as the team was his first priority. Rohit loosed the backing support of many of his key players due to injuries. Despite of having so many reasons to loose and just few reasons to win, the skipper came back with his army in style as they later won 9 out of their 10 matches that led MI to qualify for Qualifier I. Thanks to some brilliant batting presentation by Rohit Sharma, Ambati Rayudu and Kieron Pollard followed by the bowling unit. After winning the Qualifier I against CSK very calmly, MI were now into the finals of the PEPSI IPL 2015.

Rohit had the opportunity to register his name into the lists of most successful IPL captains and the skipper led from the front. Batting first MI loosed Parthiv Patel very early but then comes ROHIT to bat at No.3 and right from the first ball he played it gave us a glimpses of something great is on the way. Rohit ended up scoring 26 ball 50 in the finals against CSK. This innings of him not only led to the victory of Mumbai but also proved that at big matches, leader have to lead from the front. He was also given as the Man of the Match. Rohit, now became the second captain after the 'CHANAKYA OF CRICKET' Mahendra Singh DHONI to win the IPL trophy twice.

Rohit in IPL 2015:-

Team: Mumbai Indians

Matches: 16

Runs: 482

Average: 34.42

Strike Rate: 144.74

Best score: 98*

100/50: 0/3

4's/6's: 41/21

Season 9 (2016):-

MI failed to defend their title in the 9th edition of the IPL. They again did not ought to a good start but the captain was in a sublime touch whenever it came for a chase. Rohit played some crucial knocks which gave Mumbai a win single handedly. Scores of 84 off 54 and 85* off 60 against KKR and RPS (Rising Pune Supergiant) respectively helped the team to come back in the tournament. In the last league match in a do or die stage, MI fought very bravely with the brilliant effort of Krunal Pandya but the quick fire knocks of Suresh Raina and Brendon McCullum knocked out the defending champions and went on to end at a 5th spot on points tally.

Rohit in IPL 2016:-

Team: Mumbai Indians

Matches: 14

Runs: 489

Average: 44.45

Strike Rate: 132.88

Best score: 85*

100/50: 0/5

4's/6's: 49/16

Season 10 (2017):-

2017, the year that just bought glory into the dockyard of Mumbai Indians. The concept of the franchise was clear now as they used "ODD YEAR WIN" theory. MI finished the season with the badge of table toppers for the first time in 10 years of IPL history. After qualifying for the finals comfortably , the skipper had the plans ready as it wasn't a new experience for him. That particular game actually tested the captaincy skills of Rohit to the most extreme level. And as we all know our Hitman is always a standout performer in every situation. The nature of Rohit is quite similar as that of water i.e whatever you add in both of them, they will mix up to that very compromisely. Rohit led his team to the victory in a very low scoring game against RPS. In a very close encounter, MI went on to win the title by just 1 run and became the first team in the history of the IPL to win the trophy thrice. This game hailed as the most thrilling match of the IPL history. With this win, Rohit became the most successful IPL captain ever.

Rohit in IPL 2017:-

Team: Mumbai Indians

Matches: 17

Runs: 333

Average: 23.78

Strike Rate: 121.97

Best score: 67

100/50: 0/3

4's/6's: 31/9

Rohit's overall IPL career:-

Team: Mumbai Indians/Deccan Chargers

Matches: 173

Innings: 168

Runs: 4493

Average: 31.86

Strike Rate: 131.02

Best score: 109*

100/50: 1/34

4's/6's: 379/184

Not Outs: 27

Rohit Sharma as a captain:-

Matches: 66

Won: 40

Loss: 26

Tie/NR: 0

Tournaments won: 5 (3 IPL and 2 CLT20)

Winning %: 60.60%

Win/Loss Ratio: 1.551

Rohit has been rated brilliantly both as a captain and a batsman. He now had a new feather joined over his cap of mastery.

Its was all about IPL that gave Rohit a platform to represent his skills with all he have mainly the captaincy. And when legends of the game appreciates you for your deeds, you know you are in a right path and have been doing right thing over the years. Rohit is just doing the same.

Some great compliments from the masters are as follows:-

"If you ask me whom do I fear most as an opposition captain, I would say Rohit Sharma. He can hurt you more than Virat." Says Gautam Gambhir (IPL Captain)

One of the finest commentator of the modern era comments:

"Bhai Rohit Sharma - The captain! ki to daad deni padegi kya kaptaani karte hai ye.. waah!!" says Aakash Chopra

During the batting of Rohit Sharma in IPL 2018, Vivek Razdaan says:

"sab jaante the inka balla goonja nahi bus maun hai...

Jis din chalega bata dega kiska baap kaun hai!!" ☺

Irfaan Pathan comments:-

"Sharma ji ka ladka bowlers se badtameezi bhi badi hi tameez se karta hai!!" and many more..

7. INITIALLY TEMPORARY AND LATER ON PERMANENT PLACE AT INTERNATIONAL SETUP

When a kid in India starts playing cricket, he straight away dreams to play for India and nothing else. Without even knowing what it will take and what will it demand, the craze is just to represent India or to be more specific encounter at the International circuit.

Rohit Sharma should have dreamt the same thing but as he would have went through the shadows of cricketing world, he must have came across about the cost of International cricket and what all it requires to reach to that level. But moving with the confidence that everything can be attained! O How??

Look at Rohit. True domination, hardwork and passion!! These are among those swords and weapons that you require to win over the battle field of your tough dreams. This guy proved it like a king!

He took his game and routine seriously while playing with whatever opportunities he had and did well almost everywhere. Whether domestic circuit, national or state cricket, Rohit whooped out from the den and had his adventure all over the park in every occasion. Due to all his efforts at initial stages, he got his maiden International call for India against Ireland in the only ODI to be played on 26th June 2007.

The following sub headings are discussed in relation to the main heading:-

A. The concept of debut and World T20 2007:-

Finally all the hard work was counting slowly for Rohit Sharma. Tagging him lucky or unlucky would be too early because in the later part of the context things have changed. Rohit moved on to make his International debut immediately in his first International tour that he did. Receiving an International cap with the number of 168 printed on the left corner was something very emotional as well as a matter of pride for the man who struggled so much to face this day. It was pleasant morning of 26th of june 2007 when Rohit, wearing the Indian jersey and dressed up as blues stepped into the Belfast Cricket Ground. I am sure that particular feeling is what he (Rohit) can only define. Not me not you no one. But it was definitely one of those moments for Rohit which he will carry under his grave.

After winning the toss, Irish were put on to bat by the visitors and were encircled into the score of 193 till their tenth batsman went off. Rohit dominated into the fielding unit with some extra energy and grabbed the crucial catch of Neil 'O' Brien who was looking fine at 52. Challenged with the target of 173 in 39 over (D/L Method), Indians were prepared for the chase. Till here we came through Rohit-'the lucky' Sharma who made a fine debut but now unfortunately it turned into Rohit-'the unlucky' Sharma.

Rohit didn't got chance to bat in that game due to the unbeaten knocks of Sourav Ganguly and Gautam Gambhir of 73* and 80* respectively taking India over the line with 9 wickets to spare. This was the way no one would ever want to happen in his debut game. But its a team sport and young Rohit understands that pretty well.

After few months, the announcement made by ICC (International Cricket Council) about the inaugural edition of the World T20 paved the way for many youngsters including Rohit. The newer format of the game was tested all over the world before the main tournament and it had some fantastic results in searching new talents. In India as well, a domestic inter state T20 competition was organised in which Rohit scored a brilliant ton against Gujarat and became the first ever Indian batsman to score a century in T20 format simultaneously presenting a powerful membership application to the Indian squad for the big tournament ahead. And when senior players like Sachin, Ganguly, Dravid, etc self withdrawn themselves from the selection, the bunch of youngsters of India had the opportunity to held themselves. Rohit too, got selected for the tournament and due to the injury held to Dinesh Karthik, he got to play his first match against England on 19th September 2007. Yes you are thinking very right the same game where Yuvraj struck Stuart Broad out of the park for 6 times in an over. It was Rohit's T20I debut as well (cap: 17).

India, batting first posted their highest T20I score of 218. Gautam Gambhir and Virender Sehwag gave India an absolute remarkable start followed by mind boggling fire made by Yuvraj Singh at the end overs. And I can bet Rohit- 'the unlucky' Sharma would never have thought that he won't get to bat in this game either. Ending the debut match with just one catch never provides you the kick, you look around for. But the very next game against the hosts South Africa, Rohit was given a chance in the playing eleven due to the unfit Yuvraj and he proved... "why the hell is he sitting in the dug-out... he needs to be right there at the 22 yards box." Hahaha its just a over excitement!! Now coming back to the topic. As the caught behind of Sehwag took place, it was now his turn to enter. It was the first time Rohit entered into the ground having assigned actually what his job is i.e. batting. Team being under pressure after loosing 3 quick and big wickets, a calm and composed mind was required at the centre and he managed it quite well and didn't disappoint.

Right from ball one, Rohit looked so confident with his batting and his elegancy in the shots described the talent him. Glorious cuts, pulls, cover-drives, down the ground and many more that too against the claws of Pollock, Ntini and Morkel was just an amazing presentation. Whoever was the evidence of that innings became his fan not only because of the unbeaten 50 he made but under what situation he made. From 33/3 to 153/5 with that last ball six as a finishing kick, a lot of credit goes to Rohit for the win against the proteas. Scoring 50* off 40 balls. A calm, composed and matured innings of RO forced the team management very heavily to offer him more chances.

Rohit again had with a major contribution scoring a quick fire 30* off 16 deliveries in the finals against Pakistan. And after this tournament which India won, many cricket experts gave a tagline which leaves me with goose bumps everytime:-

"ROHIT SHARMA – THE NEXT BIG THING IN INDIAN CRICKET!!"

Trust me I still got it.

During an interview with Gaurav Kapoor, Virat Kohlli says: We used to hear everywhere we go that this player is arriving.... Rohit Sharma is coming, next big thing and all. After hearing this we used to be both curious as well as jealous to hear his name only... we were also youngsters but no one was taking our name. And then once I saw Rohit Sharma batting in T20 world cup 2007 and I was like just sit down and enjoy and from that day we came to understand that why people were taking his name only and not ours.

He adds: **"When we saw him play, we came to know what people are talking about and what we are witnessing..... AMAZING!!**

I haven't seen someone time the ball better than him."

Later on when Gaurav says: **"He (Rohit) has one second more time than other players."**

Virat interrupts: **"Not one second sir, one point five (1.5s)**

B. Major ups and downs:-

I believe every single person in this world doesn't progress on a same graph throughout his career. There are ups and downs, positives and negatives in everyone's life which naturally test their character and temperament. But its the time when you need to be very much patient and wait for the perfect time to strike yourself harder.

Similar story is of Rohit Sharma. He had a great start to his International cricket with flying colours winning off the first tournament he played and being a well contributer in that tournament with his batting just gives a bit more clinch of spice in the satisfaction he had. But what next? 'You can't always succeed', its a rule of nature that is applicable on all of us. Rohit went back with some dreams to alter his nights. After spending some moments in re-living the tournament victory, he got selected for the ODI series against Pakistan in 2007. After winning the series, team management decided to have some changes with Rohit back in the playing eleven in the 5th ODI at Jaipur. In that game, chasing more than 300, Rohit scored his maiden half century with 52 off 61 balls though he could not take his team home.

Some good and solid knocks of Rohit got him selected in the squad for the CB Series 2007-08 (Commonwealth Bank Series) in Australia. On 3rd February 2008, he got to feature in the opening game against the Aussies. He, there, couldn't do much as he would have wanted only putting a 65 run stand with Gautam Gambhir before being cleaned off through a fine edge caught back by Gilchrist ending his craft on 29. In the next game against Sri Lanka, Rohit' s story of disappointing others as well as himself continues, this time he goes back for a duck scaring India at 83/4.

4th match of the series ladies and gentlemen, Rohit with another chance, and he popped up with his match winning innings of 39* off 61 taking team India to victory alongside MS chasing a score of 160 against the hosts. Despite of a slow and disappointing start in the series, Rohit felt a lot more confident with his batting. He scored a half ton very next game ahead SL and maintained a well required partnership of 64 with Gautam Gambhir and then a quick fire of 68 with Dhoni. Though India didn't came up as a winning side, Rohit did fair to his potentials by scoring 70* off 64 with those 2 crucial partnership as well. 7th game, downfall again. Rohit with just 1 under his belt on this occasion followed by 24, 1 and 3* in the next three encounters.

Now it was a big 1st final of CB Series, India vs Australia. The pressure of league games and knockouts are completely different. Rohit got chances unexpectedly and now he had to give up with something Wowwww!! And that's what he did. Combining a match winning partnership with his idol, Sachin. The duo joined 123 big runs with Rohit of 66 as his individual score. It was this pair probably which took India over the line in the first final at SCG (Sydney Cricket Ground). Oops moment again in the 2nd finals with just 2 runs ahead of RG Sharma.

After these few series Rohit played, cricket pundits came across his potential and what atmosphere he can set when he gets going. Time passed and so on. Rohit by this time having with many ups and downs in his career. Whenever he wanted to rise the mountain of consistency, the 'inconsistency' evil with scary face used to pull his legs and bring him back. Rohit played some good knocks and had good start in many games but all of a sudden he does something really extra ordinary that results in throwing away his wicket leaving us Oh No!! What's the need of this yaarr....!! This was the very reason behind not capitalising some good starts. After observing this process of wasting talent and opportunities, a cricket journalist, Harsha Bhogle mentions:- **" every single time that I watch Rohit Sharma bat, my joy drops at the quality of one or two shots he plays and then I throw my head back at frustration because he just does something you would imagine why.......**

Why he had thrown his wicket away!!"

Rohit was a good performer but the fact also wasn't wrong that he was highly inconsistent.

He scored his maiden International hundred on 28th may 2010, 3 years since his intl. debut. He played a solid knock of 114 against Zimbabwe at Queens Sports Club. Followed up with amazing another ton against Sri Lanka remaining not out at 101*at the same venue few days later. But yet another downfall. Yes we all know that in the game of cricket you can't hit centuries on a trot but the encyclopaedia of the game says if you want a medal of 'consistent', you have to score 30 to 40 odd runs in every game and after 3 to 4 innings have to convert that odd runs to a three figure mark. By this theory only you can be counted among the brilliants in the game. Getting 50 to 60 runs after a long period of time wont work in the International circuit as there are so many contenders behind you waiting for an opportunity to grab your slot. But team support and their belief was one of the biggest positives that he took all the time along with him when he walked into the ground. Rohit faced many ups and downs since his debut (2007) till 2012 before the turning point of his career came and said him, Hello!! I am success. Lets hug up for forever!!

This particular column [7,B] can be also named or titled as "ROHIT – MAN OF MASTERCLASS 1.O."

ROHIT – INCONCISTENNT SHARMA'S ODI career till 2012:-

Innings: 81

Runs: 1978

Average: 30.43

Strike Rate: 77.93

100's/50's: 2/12

Best Score: 144 vs Zimbabwe

"You have to accept there will be failures but you have to work throughout it" - Rohit Sharma.

C. Criticisms and trolling:-

Criticism is a very small word but what impact it can had on a particular character is enormous. It has couple of aspects both negative as well as positive. Just depends on the person how and on what note he takes it and how he responds to that. Reacting towards the world is absolutely useless in fact if he reacts towards himself that would give him a better result and I firmly believe that there are too many stray dogs that barks when a elephant crosses the street but its up to him that how it takes those shouts. The giant elephant just ignores all and keeps on walking on his way. The same attitude needs to be carried out by all of us to survive I this world.

C for Cricketers and C for Criticism. They are among the best changu mangu who never leaves each others hand. Come on, name me a cricketer ever who isn't criticised at all?? None!! And in this segment Rohit Sharma have been featuring since a long period of time. The kind of humiliation that he had went through is so much de-motivating and loosing support. Rohit, since his debut, due to his inconsistency and a bit margin of error in the shot selection, have been a medium for the people to criticise. Not only for the people who are not well known about cricket but for the cricket pundits (experts) as well. They have not let away a single chance go to criticise this man and I don't know why.. may be some other reasons behind it.

But Rohit, as a player or to be more specific as a sports person and myself as his fan cum writer, we both believe that its a very necessary part of a game. It gives you that mental challenge to prove others how good you are and to say on their face 'you were wrong'. The previous sub heading of this section [7B] is pretty much related to this sub heading [7C]. Ups and downs → failure → criticism → challenge → hard work → success!

('→' means 'leads to')

This algorithm can be proved right by no one else but Rohit Sharma. At the moment of time all the supporters of Rohit used to believe that his haters may have got some particular reason for hatredness towards him. But later on both Rohit and myself would like to thank all those who put a question mark on his ability. Its because of you all guys we got our inspiration and idol and our love got so much of success and fame.

Sometimes I even think if all those things that Rohit was bearing early in his career several years back comes up to me or if I would been there at his place then what I would have done? May be I would have never picked up that bat and kit again or any such thing. The humiliating statements from the legends of the game was enough to put a exit way in his cricketing career but the determination owed by Rohit didn't allowed him to visit or even think towards that exit way.

Harsha Bhogle, a cricket journalist and Rohit Sharma fan now, then says:-

"That is how Rohit Sharma is. You tell him he played badly and he will tell you that Manish Pandey played even more badly. I don't know if he is a human being. How can a human waste so many opportunities

Another big player from SA, says:-

"If you really want to see a wasted talent, look into Rohit Sharma' s eyes" - AB Devilliers

New Zealand's bowler and Rohit's teammate, Tim Southee comments:-

"Try to take his (Rohit) wicket in the first five minutes. If you cant, then don't worry he will throw his wicket himself"

World's No.1 bowler Mitchell Starc had with his view:-

"If you cant get Rohit's wicket, you're struggling in your career."

Not only from cricketing world but criticisms held from everywhere including bollywood as a director/producer, Karan Johar says:-

"Rohit Sharma is to cricket is what Harman Baweja is to bollywood."

But if someone asks me what is success, I will show them these couple of statements from the universe boss, Chris Gayle regarding Rohit Sharma:-

"Rohit Sharma could get out like me but I Could never get out like him" - Chris Gayle, few years back.

"I am always a fan of Rohit Sharma and I always tell him he is one of the best player I have actually seen in India" - Chris Gayle at Ceat Cricket Awards 2018.

Within these two statements of CH Gayle, the whole journey of Rohit Sharma can be estimated. But it is a phase that every cricketer had to go through. You cant escape from being criticised and trolled everywhere. Its a kind of march in which every viewer participates without knowing the reason for it but no one objects if it is wrong. We all came across our view but I think its quite necessary to have the view of that person about whom this book has been written.

When Rohit was asked by a fan during the EXPRESSADDA interview that:-

"The media uses you all the time. First they will call you stylish, beautiful to watch, this and that and suddenly two innings kharab ho gaya, doesn't live up

to the potential. So you are a great folder for a people in media to write great columns and use that material and this happens only with good looking players. Do you sometimes feel that if I would have lesser good looking person then whatever you could have done, it would have been rocky??"

After this Rohit – the sarcastic Sharma replies:-

"You said correctly. I have given a lot to many people to talk about. Many people have actually sustained their job because of me by writing articles on me when they had nothing to do. That's how it goes. So I am happy about it that I am helping someone in some or the other way."

In an another interview again in CNBCTV18, he was asked with the criticism segment of his life.

"For every sports person, it comes challenging time when you stop performing or when you under perform. People pick out the faults in you and criticise you. How do you carry the weight of billions expectations on your shoulders??"

Rohit answers:-

"By now I am used to with it. Earlier I wasn't. I used to react, I used to stress about this a lot before. But now with experience, I have understood that what matters is your time on the field and it gives you the opportunity to go and do something for your nation. Rather than thinking about what XYZ are talking about my game, its pointless. Because what matters at the end of the day is what you do on the field. You will fail sometimes also. As a cricketer, I have limited time in my career and I want to enjoy that time rather than thinking about Oo what is he saying about me and remember not everyone gets to play for India and the pride of wearing India crest. So why not to stay and be proud of that!

This book wouldn't have been written if Rohit had given upon these tough situations and criticisms. The fight to gain some respect is what shows your dedication. Once again on behalf of Rohit, I would like to say a heartiest thank you to all the criticizers that they burnt up the hunger and fire in him to stand where he is today.

D. Too much disappointment:-

This particular column can be clarified with just a couple of incidents which gave a plenty of disappointment to Rohit Shrama. In the year 2010, after becoming a well experienced limited over player, Rohit was all ready to be launched in 5 days cricket as well. When VVS Laxman failed to recover from his injury before the 1st test match of South Africa tour of India back in February 2010, Rohit was all set to begin the journey of 'whites' now that too on his home turf of Nagpur. But fate had different plans and no one can change it. Few hours before the start of play in the morning, Rohit injured himself while playing football during warm up and had to sit due to injury. After this he didn't got the opportunity and had to wait three years to make his test debut.

On this particular disappointment, Rohit says:-

"I don't want to remember that incident. Biggest disappointment of my life as I had to wait three years to make my debut."

This was a huge disappointment for him and who would have thought that its not over yet as it was followed by yet another throwback the very next year. Back to back disappointments was a huge drawback in Rohit's career.

Every player who picks up the cricket equipment in his hands wants to play at international level as discussed in the previous contents but if we keep that dream aside and think for a couple of moments that what he will dream or he dreams after he gets this opportunity of playing international cricket. May be of playing the biggest tournament in the world that is 'World Cup'.

Rohit dreamt the same. He was getting chances on a regular note to prove his skills and to some extent he didn't let the chances go but the only obstacle that blocked his way was 'inconsistency'. Due to this reason he wasn't rated on heights as his team members were.

Making the debut in 2007, Rohit must be determined and focussed towards the upcoming ICC World Cup 2011 and what made it taste more sweeter was the venue of the tournament as it was to be played in the subcontinent with India as a leading host. This was an alarm for the young talents of India to make their places to the team. Rohit was consistently offered opportunities after the CB series 07-08. Despite of being inconsistent and unable to score big, the team management backed him to the extreme but having scored 5,1,23,9,11, DNB,44,5,11,00,4 in his last 10 innings before a huge tournament doesn't link up to qualify for the selection and Rohit would have never thought that his dreams would shatter in such a manner. There was no Rohit Sharma in the 15 mans squad for the World Cup 2011. Dream to play World Cup was yet to come true for him. Piyush Chawla, who hasn't played a single ODI in India was given priority before Rohit. So much of disappointment. To miss a big tournament like World Cup that too on the home conditions and soil was really a huge miss for Rohit and a devasted feeling. It seemed that everything is over for Rohit Sharma.

The statement given by Rohit after being excluded from the WC squad signifies his pain and disappointment as he says:-

"It was the biggest jolt, I received in my life. Its a pain I cannot explain. My teammates would be playing cricket's biggest tournament on home soil and all I'll be doing will watch them on TV. It hurts me so much."

But there is a very famous proverb that "whatever happens, it happens for a good sake". The heart break of Rohit led to more dedication and hardwork which was a way to success for Rohit as he never gave up!!

E. 'Hard' work turns to 'Hardest':-

When you get disappointment and face troubles in your career, its a notice that wakes you up and informs to double the hard work. No doubt, you would have worked very hard to give a strong representation of yours but when you don't end up succeeding in that then make sure its the time when you have to rebuild your dreams and pave a way towards it. Double the hard work you did, triple the confidence you possessed and multiply the belief in yourself and you will find soon success and fame will knock your door.

After being ignored for the World Cup 2011, Rohit was very depressed with the results and with no one else but himself. I don't know what Rohit's thinking would have been at that point of time but I would just stand on my feet applauding his dedication and the mindset of not giving up at any situation. Rohit may have easily quit the way which many of us might have done at that time but he re-built his dreams and after learning tough lessons moved on a journey to rediscover himself. When Rohit was thinking about all these stuffs, once at night, Yuvraj Singh took out him for a dinner in which he explained everything that was going through Rohit's mind. He gave him with the boost that he required the most. Making him count his faults, what he needs to improve, on what department he needs to work hard, etc. etc. After this effort of Yuvi regarding

Rohit, it gave him the confidence to dream again. First of all the moves, he had to forget what all happened within the past few days and just to focus on the future.

He joined gym sessions, paid attention on his fitness and made attempts to improve his batting and cricketing skills. The hard work of Rohit showed the frustration inside him and the shock that he got some days back. One of his Mumbai teammates, Abhishek Nayar, says:- **"He slogged with me in the gym and transformed into a hard-working cricketer".**

Former Mumbai coach, Pravin Amre, was left amazed after seeing the efforts Rohit was putting to improve himself as a cricketer:-

"He improved his fitness and became more mature and responsible."

Rohit, in the action of being improved as much as he can, talked to his coach Dinesh Lad and spent some time under his guidance and coaching. After looking at Rohit's approach Dinesh says:-

"He was really depressed that time when he was dropped from the World Cup squad. But eventually that proved to be the best thing that happened to him. It made him focus on the game a lot more.

I'll come back into the Indian team with a bang, **he told me. His game changed completely. He started capitalizing on his starts and became a completely different player."**

Rohit's view on the hard work he did after being excluded from the World Cup squad:-

"I have nothing to prove to anyone. I have to prove it to myself that I am much more capable than what I have done so far. When I look into the mirror, I

should be able to look into my eyes and talk to myself about my achievements."

He worked hard to get into the Indian team but worked the hardest to cement his place in the Indian team. We could probably say that by this time 'Rohit Sharma 2.0' was a bit visible and 'Rohit Sharma 1.0' was getting disappeared. Rohit's hard work that turned hardest was one of the reasons behind success.

F. Turning point of the career:-

After fighting through so much of troubles and having done too much hard work, Rohit was now expecting the rewards for it. But you need to have some opportunities which Rohit already had several times before. Immediately after the World Cup 2011, Rohit was again joined in the Indian team but this time as an opener than a middle order blast taking a hope of may fates turn around. Now Rohit was charged into the opening slot. Under the captainship of MS Dhoni, Rohit opened the innings for the very first time in his career. But you cant hope that your experiment may turn right in the first attempt itself. Rohit started giving good starts to his team in most of the matches he opened. He scored his first half century (83) as an opener against England at Mohali on 23rd Jan 2013 in the 4th match of England tour of India. Again in the tour of South Africa, he was given with the role to open but he had a horrible tour there averaging in around fifteens. The questions again began to rise on his place in the team and about his technique to play the outside off deliveries. But the team management had plenty of belief in him mainly the captain.

The turning point of his career came in June 2013 during the ICC Champions Trophy. Rohit being included in that particular squad initially found it difficult to search his place as the opening order was fixed with Murali Vijay and

Shikhar Dhawan featuring in that list. But MS Dhoni decided to play Rohit as a regular opener and after this decision everything literally changed. The flow of wind which once used to be against Rohit's favour now flew under his feets. 6th June 2013, first game of the tournament, IND vs SA. Rohit playing as an opener was not new with this position but was quite nervous. As he walked into bat, he knew its enough now, he had to deliver. Despite of starting slow, as Rohit was timing the ball better, the confidence meter was getting high. After playing some fabulous cricketing shots, he ended his innings on 65 off 81 deliveries. Most importantly he gave his team a good start than his own performance. After this innings he never looked back. He had fine tournament further scoring 52, 18, 33 and 9 against WI, PAK, SL and ENG respectively in tough overcast conditions.

This tournament was probably the turning point in Rohit's career and MS was the one who'll get the full credit for it.

When he was asked why he choosed Rohit as an opener, he replies:-

"He wasn't getting enough opportunities to bat. He used to bat at no. 6 due to our fixed top and middle order which we felt was a bit waste of talent. So we decided to make him an opener because he cuts and pulls well and he is natural stroke player again which to some extents helps the team because once he gets going, he can play long innings."

Rohit ended up that tournament being the 4th highest run getter overall and 2nd for India.

Here are his stats:-

Matches/Innings: 5

Runs: 177

Average: 35.40

Highest Score: 65 against SA, Cardiff

At the end of this tournament, Rohit Sharma 2.0 completely took over the older him. Lets know what Rohit himself says about this move:-

"When MS asked me to open the innings, I straihght away agreed to do so and if he could have asked me to bat no. 6 then also I would have agreed because at that point of time I just wanted to play and yes that

decision of MS to make me open changed my career. After that move I became a better player. Now I can understand my game very well and I believe that this particular move was the turning point of my career."

Here are some of the stats that prove Rohit's thinking right.

Rohit as an opener:-

Innings: 95

Runs:- 4627

Average: 53.80

100's/50's: 15/22

Strike Rate:- 91.10

Highest Score:- 264

These stats are those which every player dreams to have. Its enough to prove what transformation did Rohit had after 2013. Since 2013, Rohit has the best average of 53.80 among all the openers in the world proving his improvement and consistency.

G. Consistent Sharma:-

The move as a regular opener was doing healthy job for Rohit Sharma as it turned around his cricket and career completely. Everything he did since then went his way. He was bagging huge number of runs in his dockyard. Almost wherever he played, he did well, giving his team a opening kick in most of the time in all type of conditions. Earlier Rohit was not paid much of attention due to his inconsistency and gifting away his wickets at crucial junctions of the game. But now slowly, he started to value his wicket and came to know what it costs to himself as well as his team.

After very few matches only, Rohit got a far better reputation in the world of cricket as compared to several years back. The most important feather for a player that is consistency, which he didn't have was now plugged into his cap. Rohit became a more consistent performer and now understood his responsibilities quite well. We witnessed a new Rohit Sharma who was doing very much justice now to his potentials.

The stats represented below will definitely prove me as well as my words correct:-

Rohit's year-wise data after being an opener in ODI:-

2013

Matches: 28

Runs: 1196

Average: 52.00

100/50: 2/8

Strike Rate: 80.81

HS: 209 vs Australia, Bengaluru

2014

Matches: 12

Runs: 578

Average: 52.55

100/50: 1/3

Strike Rate: 94.29

HS: 264 vs Sri Lanka, Kolkata

2015

Matches: 17

Runs: 815

Average: 50.94

100/50: 3/4

Strike Rate: 95.43

HS: 150 vs South Africa, Kanpur

<u>2016</u>

Matches: 10

Runs: 564

Average: 62.67

100/50: 2/2

Strike Rate: 95.27

HS: 171* vs Australia, Perth

<u>2017</u>

Matches: 21

Runs: 1293

Average: 71.83

100/50: 6/5

Strike Rate: 99.46

HS: 208* vs Sri Lanka, Mohali

<u>2018</u>

Matches: 6*

Runs: 115

Average: 28.23

100/50: 1/0

Strike Rate: 82.93

HS: 115 vs South Africa, Port Elzabeth

As you will come through these stats, you will find that his average did not came below 50 a single time except the incomplete edition of 2018 which determines his top class consistency which took him to the title of 'THE ONE DAY MONSTER!'

H. Test Cricket Influence:-

There was a time when test cricket itself opened its arms to welcome Rohit but due to injury his entrance in those lap of white ball cricket was postponed. He was all set to make debut in test cricket but injured his ankle minutes before the play. And he would never have imagined that he will get the next chance 3 years later. The likes of Cheteshwar Pujara and Virat Kohli urged ahead of Rohit. But again due to his good performance in ODI cricket, he was selected for the West Indies tour of India in 2013 which was Sachin's farewell test series as well.

Despite of averaging 60.03 in First Class cricket and carrying enough experience of 6 years of International Cricket, it was going to be very challenging for Rohit to adjust himself to the red ball cricket. It had different demands from other formats. Rohit played his first test match at Eden Gardens and this time luckily being completely fit and fine. The way he took off, it seemed that he will really go high ending his career being one of the greats of this format. He went on to score a century in his debut innings becoming one of the few Indians to score a hundred on debut. His score of 177 was the second highest score on debut by an Indian after his ODI partner Shikhar Dhawan. Followed by another ton at his home ground, Wankhede, in the very next match remaining not out at 111*. Rohit was ragging the selectors for not selecting him in the past tours.

But since this time, the graph went very low and did not came up till now. After his first few innings, Rohit was onto a Run strike. He scored his first 2 centuries in 2013 and had to wait for 4 long year to celebrate his 3rd ton in 2017. Rohit till now, hasn't proved himself as a pronounced test cricketer which was disappointing for all cricket lovers. Given with such a plenty of chances to prove, whether its SA, AUS, NZ or anywhere, he failed to leave an impact in the white jersey and had to struggle almost wherever he played.

In a recent interview, when Rohit was asked about his selection in the test team, he answers:-

"There's a limited time you have as a player and I have finished almost half of it. There's no point spending the remaining half thinking whether I'll be picked or not. I am going forward with the theory of whatever time I have, make it count."

Rohit in test cricket:-

Matches: 25

Runs: 1479

Average: 39.97

100's/50's: 3/9

HS: 177 vs West Indies, Kolkata

I. E'den'- The Den for Rohit:-

Every cricketer carry some sort of extra confidence when they walk into a particular ground. The confidence that leads to only destruction for bowlers and audience. Similar habit is of Rohit too. Whenever he comes to this city, he doesn't bring any nervousness with him. Or may be due to the habit of forgetting serious things, he may have forgot to bring that along with him. The time whenever he has walked into the eden gardens, we have witnessed something absolute unforgettable. Rohit just loves to play and bat here due to the crowd factor. The way he play or just by observing his body language, it seems that he is playing a game against the block B of his society at the backyard of his building. This combo is so destructive that I would suggest a board to be hanged outside the gates with the warning 'BOWLERS!! DO NOT ENTER!!'.

The first ever meeting of this couple came back in 2008 during the first IPL season when Rohit represented Deccan Chargers and was ready to play against KKR at Eden. He was swapped off for a duck by Karthik. But this was just one of those quiet periods which indicated a heavy storm ahead. The first major juncture between Rohit and Eden came up in 2013 when he got to his maiden IPL hundred here. And then later on the season brought a glory for him as under his captaincy MI crowned their first IPL trophy at Eden. After the beginning, it never came to an end whether we talk about Rohit's 177 against WI on his test debut or three IPL championship, it wont end. But what stands to the top of the list was the knock of 264 against SL. Coming back from an injury, Rohit went on to score the highest individual score in limited overs format. This ground has turned the fates for hitman whenever he gets his steps inside it.

A little boy asked Rohit how he scores so many runs playing at Eden Gardens. Rohit replies:-

"Eden Gardens is my favourite. I don't know things just fall in place there. I get that feel good factor when I enter Eden Gardens, everytime I play. Every player has that one particular stadium where they just go and feel at home so I feel that way when I go to Eden."

In the last nine innings at the Eden Gardens, Rohit has scored 794 runs at an envious strike rate and average of 99.87 and 113 respectively across all formats including IPL. These numbers are enough to show how transparent Rohit used to be when he is at E'den' Gardens.

8. ATTAINMENT OF TITLE 'HITMAN'.

Well many of us knows about the concept of discovery of the title hitman but I am very sure that most of you would be going through misconception. Many fans and peoples believe that it was none other than Ravi Shashtri who gave rise to this name but my dear friends if you are going that way then let me turn you wrong.

The match was in Jaipur, IND vs AUS. India was asked to chase a target 350 plus which later on they were successful to chase under the glamour of Virat and Rohit. After that game, a guy called PD in the crew came to Rohit and said 'you played like a Hit-man.' So eventually it was him who discovered this name and I would say Rohit too deserved this name because he is the Hitman of world cricket. We can't find anyone as perfect as Rohit fits with this tag. But this title was brought to all of us by one of the finest commentator Ravi Shashtri when he comments:-

"He goes inside out and what a way to bring up 200 in One Day Internationals. They call him HITMAN and he is arrived into the party.

An outstanding double hundred (200) for Rohit Sharma"

After Rohit gets to his first ODI double hundred.

The other nicknames that Rohit carries 'Ro', 'Shaana, etc.

Rohit personally verifies by explaining:-

"It happened in 2013 when I was playing against Australia at Bangalore. There is a guy called PD in the crew, he said after the game at Jaipur that 'you played like a hitman.' Ravi bhai was standing there, heard it and said it during commentary. I think it caught up like that."

9. PERSONAL LIFE (MARRIAGE, ETC)

Whenever we say 'personal' about a celebrity or a cricket icon like Rohit Sharma, the first thought that crawls through our mind is that of marriage. Yes, in this particular content we are going to talk about Rohit's personal life including his wedding as well.

Going back to past few years. Before being tied up, they already knew each other for a fine 6 years. Rohit and Ritika met as a professionals very first time during a Ad shoot in which Ritika was a sports event manager. After the first eye contact, Rohit guessed the lady to be the boasting one and have proud sort of attitude and soon he receives a warning from Yuvraj singh not to try anything on her as she was his sister. Time went on passing since then and Ritika started managing Rohit's cricket life as well. They used to meet at regular periods with some improvements in their relationship status everytime they met. Initially for work and then as friends and then as best friends which very soon turned into love. Both of them decided to take their relationship a step ahead.

The IPL season was on. After knowing each other very well, Rohit decided to propose Ritika very surprisingly. It was a night before his birthday. He asked Ritika to join him outside for an ice cream treat. The couples went out in a car in which Rohit played Ritika's favourite song and came up to Borivali by driving. Ritika wasn't able to understand anything and what was going infront of her. Rohit then took her to a very special place, Borivali Sports Club, the place where Rohit started his career at 11. Rohit followed the bollywood style of proposing and went on to knees with a solitaire ring in his hands and popped the proposal to her. Ritika as a normal lady, felt so special when a guy like Rohit Sharma proposed her in a way that every girls dreams of. Tears shed from her eyes and the duo went on to get engaged on 3rd June 2015.

Since then begins a beautiful love story of Mr and Mrs Sharma. Both of them merged up to signify one soul on 13th of December 2015. The wedding took place at Mumbai's Taj Lands Hotel. All the mega star of cricket, bollywood and business visited to bless the couples for the immense love they possess. Now both were tied up for the upcoming 7 births (according to myth) by promising to be there whenever they need each other. And in this our Rohit got converted to Ritika's Ro.

Its been three years since their wedding and Ritika has followed Rohit like a shadow over the years. No, not on a negative thought but to support him wherever he played. The love that she shows by crossing her fingers since Rohit starts batting and not opening it till he departs is unconditional. This shows how much this lady care for her husband. Whether its IPL or International, whatever Rohit did, Ritika was always there to stand ahead of him in his success and lag behind him in his failures and kept on motivating Rohit to do well. She says, **"He (Rohit) is the strongest person I know and I am proud of him."**

Here are some favourites of Rohit:-

Favourite team to play against: Australia

Favourite Shot: Pull Shot

Favourite ground: Eden Gardens

Favourite cricketer: Sachin Tendulkar

Favourite Food: Proper Mumbai Street Food, Chinese

Hobbies: Travelling, watching movies, sleeping

Favourite Actor: Hritik Roshan, Jeremy Piven

Favourite Actress: Kareena Kapoor

Favourite Film: Veer-Zara, The Avengers, Iron Man

Favourite Director: David Dhawan, James Cameron

Favourite Franchise: Real Madrid (Football)

Favourite Car: Aston Martin

Favourite Hotel: Long Beach Golf

Favourite Destination: Mauritius

Favourite Non Cricket Sports Personality: Zinedine Zidane

Cars Collection: BMW M5 Series

- He is a firm believer of Lord Ganesha and mostly visits Siddhivinayak temple before any tour.
- He once said that he struggles to bat against Brett Lee.
- He doesn't smoke but consume alcohol occasionally
- If not Cricketer, he would have been a Real Estate Businessman.

Note: The information shared above have been collected through Google and some recent Interviews of Rohit. In case you find anything wrong, You can have me with my Mail ID shared in the author's profile. (most of the info's are correct)

10. LOVE AFFAIR WITH MIGHTY DOUBLE HUNDREDS (200'S)

If we go around couple of decades back and talk about a double hundred score individually, then people may advice us to visit some neuron specialist. Because at that time it was beyond the imagination world that anyone can score a double ton of his own in limited overs cricket. But its true now, we have a total of 5 men cricketers who have made us the witness of their double hundreds. The trend was started by none other than but the 'God' himself, Mr. Sachin Ramesh Tendulkar when he did something literally unexpected at Gwalior in 2010. 24th of February against SA, he became the first person on the planet to score 200 in ODI cricket. If the 'Guru' does something how can it be possible the 'Chela' stay behind. After a year, Virender Sehwag followed Sachin and went on to score the previous highest individual score of 219 in ODI. But the man who carried this trend to next topmost level was sublime 'Rohit Sharma: The king of 200's.'

The kind of acceleration this human does after his century mark is something out of this world and this accelerating strength is the reason behind that he has got 3 double centuries in One Day Internationals whether no one has got even 2. He carries the world record of the highest individual score of 264 in limited overs game. Rohit believes all his 200's came at the crucial times when the team needed it the most. Lets tabulate this fact:-

209 vs Australia, 2nd Nov 2013, Bangalore:-

The series decider. But personally, Rohit had already proven himself in the series as an opener but he had to stand out for his team to lift up the Border-Gavaskar Trophy. India put on to bat first. Rohit was utilising all the confidence that he got previously in that series. But after getting Virat run out at the crucial point, was something Rohit was depressed of. But moving forward he got to his century in the 38th over. Virat stood up clapping for his mate forgetting whatever happened on the ground. It wasn't over yet. Rohit completed his century off 114 balls and no one would have even thought that by the end of the innings he will get to another hundred which came at an incredible pace. The second hundred came off just 44 deliveries. This was an unbelievable stuff from Hitman. Since then he got addicted to 200's.

Runs: 209

Balls: 158

4's/6's: 12/16

Strike Rate: 132.27

A. 264 vs SL, 13th Nov 2014, Eden Gardens:-

The 4th ODI of the series. Rohit was making a comeback after a series and it is never easy to come back from an injury and score big straight away. During the initial stages of the inning, he was struggling too much. Nothing was going in his way whether its feet movement or timing the ball, Rohit was facing difficulty in all the departments. After being dropped for 4, slowly Rohit got back his timing and played some good shots that helped him to build up his innings. He gets his century anyhow in the 32nd over facing 99 balls and celebrates it in style because he knew how difficult it was for him to get to that. And then suddenly a tweet flashes on the social media of MS Dhoni, the Astrologer saying "if Rohit doesn't get out he will certainly get 250 today". This turned as a true one. Rohit got to his second double hundred in 153 balls with scoring the most number of fours in that innings. But this time the stoppage of Rohit Express was a bit extended as the mumbaikar went on to score 250 becoming the first ever man to do so. Going back with the tag of highest individual score ever in the limited over cricket was something memorable for Rohit.

Runs: 264

Balls: 153

4's/6's: 33/9

Strike Rate: 152.60

B. 208* vs SL, 13th Dec 2017, PCA Mohali:-

This was again a crucial match for the team as they lost the first match of the series at Dharamshala and Rohit as a captain had to lead from the front in the second game. And what he did, only he can do that. It was now a habit for Rohit to convert 100 to 200. He again went on to score a beautiful hundred off 115 balls and completed it in the 40th over. Just imagine... he scored 100 runs under his own name in the last 60 balls to spare. By knowing this you can estimate the destruction that may have happened all over the park. When Rohit goes in this way, the 22 yards pitch turns into a graveyard for the opponent's bowlers. Second hundred again came of just 38 balls with a strike rate of 282 which proved he is a lone warrior of this race. No one can even get closer to the level that Rohit has set in terms of acceleration and conversion.

Runs: 208*

Balls: 153

4's/6's: 13/12

Strike Rate: 135.94

Other than these 3 double hundreds, Rohit has scored 150+ scores 5 times in ODI format equalling the record of David Warner and Sachin Tendulkar. And those 5 innings are:-

264 off 153 against SL, Eden 2013

209 off 158 against Aus, Bangalore 2014

208* off 153 against SL, Mohali 2017

171* off 163 against Aus, WACA Perth 2016

150 off 133 against SA, Kanpur 2015

These are also the highest individual score for India in ODI's in the last 5 years. And the facts that prove why no one else can do what Rohit does are stated below:-

1. He has the best strike rate between 43 and 50 overs in ODIs since 2013. (254.31)
2. He has hit the 3rd most number of sixes between 43 and 50 overs in ODIs since 2013. (20)
3. He has the 2nd best average between 43 and 50 overs in ODIs since 2013. (59.00)

Rohit's pace at different stages of the innings:-

Over range	Ave	SR	Dot%	4's/6's%
First 10	40.35	66.8	66.68%	59.70%
11th-27th	63.60	82.5	49.18%	43.19%
28th-43rd	83.29	130.1	35.96%	60.03%
44th-50th	59.00	254.3	14.66%	81.36%

Rohit Sharma changing gears:-

Score	SR	Balls/Bound.	Balls/ 6's
0-100	94.4	9.2	42.7
100+	184.8	3.6	9.7

Rohit in last 16 innings when he scored ODI hundred:

Score Range	Runs	BF	SR	B/F	B/6
<=50	811	987	80.3	10.6	75.9
>50, <=100	802	721	107.3	7.8	26.7
>100	767	415	184.8	3.6	9.7
Overall	2380	2123	112.1	7.1	25.6

Since 2001 in ODIs, Rohit has scored most number of runs after scoring a hundred and his average score when he scores a ODI hundred is 148.75, highest in the world. He has the best average of 72.62 batting first in ODIs since 2013.

A question was asked to Virender Sehwag that **"who has the guts in the Indian Team to complete fifties and hundreds with sixes like you?"**

Sehwag answers:

"No one was there but now we have Sharma.. Rohit Sharma!!"

Similarly Sanjay Manjrekar compliments Rohit:

"Rohit Sharma proves you don't need to be fit and have big muscles to hit effortless sixes."

11. RESOPNSIBILITIES OF HIS TEAM

The whole world has quite a famous saying that when a person is handed over with a little responsibility then probably most out of him comes out. The person starts understanding his worth and values.

Rohit Sharma used to bat at middle order in his young career and we all know his numbers were not doing at all justice with the potentials he had. But as soon as he was handed with the responsibility of his team on his shoulders, a different character came into limelight since then. He was given two big tasks in 2013. First one came during the IPL when he was given with the captaincy keys of Mumbai Indians and after that he turned into a completely different player both as a batsman as well as a captian. And second time during the ICC Champions Trophy 2013 when he was assigned with the new role of opening the innings and he had around 20% burden of his team. Burden to give his team a good start everytime he opens. These two changes when granted to Rohit, he emerged as a stand out performer not only for the Indian team but from wherever he played. That particular year of 2013 changed Rohit to Ro-hit.

Rohit knew the value of this very well. Its such honour for anyone when his team relies on him not completely but to some extent. The team believes that this particular person is capable enough to carry us and our responsibilities. Rohit too feels proud when this thought is put into action. Rohit as an opener is the best in the world whereas Rohit as an captain can be the best in the world if he is given some regular situations to use his captaincy skills. He has the 2nd highest success rate of 63.33% as a captain in the world after Shoaib Malik. He became the first captain to win IPL thrice in 2017. He is the only captain in the world whose team have never lost a tournament final, they played.

When it comes to blue jersey, Rohit got the honour to captain India in December 2017 against Sri Lanka. After this experience Rohit says, **" day that I will remember for the rest of my life. Walking out with the team sheet for the first time was a feeling of its own which can never be measured or compared with anything. Proud to be playing with the guys who have such great skill set & work ethic. Cannot be more happier."** Though India lost the first game under the captaincy debut of Rohit Sharma, they went on to win both the ODI and T20 series against SL. After few months, Rohit took India to the top in the Nidahas Trophy 2018, picking up the cup.

Therefore, I personally believe that responsibilities polished the skills of Rohit Sharma and due to these pressure, today his shine can be observed from miles away.

Rohit as Captain:-

Format	Matches	Wins	Loss	Win%
T20+IPL	90	57	32	63.33%
ODIs	03	02	01	66.66%
Tests	–	–	–	–

Rohit as Batsman:-

First 81 innings:

Runs: 1978 Ave: 30.43 Centuries: 02

Next 81 innings:

Runs: 4055 Ave: 55.31 Centuries: 15

12. A REPUTED AND WELL MAINTAINED CRICKETER

If you ask any of the cricket fan around the globe that 'who is Rohit Sharma?' and he denies to recognise then there must be two outputs. Either he is not a cricket fan or he is lying to the top most level. Rohit Sharma is a name that was registered into the cricket dictionary 11 years back in 2007 but got an asterisk (*) of important ones after 2013. He has an establish reputation in the cricketing world. Due to his hardwork and solid performances, he has set such an surrounding where everyone takes his name with full respect which he truly deserves. Not all, at the same time you have haters as well who don't like your success and attitude which is their problem because that day will never come when you wont have a single hater. The numbers of haters you have determines how you have improved over the years and attained success in your career.

Rohit is one of those very few cricketers in the world who doesn't have a single controversy to his name around the social media or anywhere. The calm, cool and composed nature of him is the reason behind the respect he earns wherever he goes. Remaining cam doesn't signify that he don't expresses his emotions. He is also a human and shows his feelings to the world. But if he is ragged by any fellow straight forward without any reason, then what happens next is his second existence. Once during the tour of Australia in 2015-16, at Adelaide when Rohit's LBW appeal for Steve Smith was denied by the umpire, Smith whispered something towards him after which Rohit with full Mumbai's attitude gave a solid reply to Steve making him realise that I am quite that doesn't mean I couldn't roar. But this incident does not prove he is arrogant and aggressive. Its a part of the game but both your nature on the field as well as off the field is taken into consideration when you are judged.

As time passed, Rohit became more silent and cooler on the ground. He believed in the policy of quietly chipping in, doing the work and moving back. Well, that's how the legends communicate and that's how they are. They don't make announcements of their good deeds they do. They are well maintained, respected all over the world and do the job quietly for their team. And Rohit Sharma is one of them!!

13. CONTRIBUTIONS OF PEOPLE WHO TURNED ROHIT TO RO-HIT

There are many personalities behind a person's success. They just remain away from the limelight that they deserve. And without the efforts of these unsung heroes, there would never been a mega star born. Behind Rohit Sharma there were too many sacrifices, love and support which made the way for him where he walks today. This content is completely dedicated to those who helped Rohit to become Ro-Hit. Though we have already discussed about them in our previous chapters, lets revise them again with a big thank you. Here are those contributions:-

1. Gurunath Sharma and Purnima Sharma (Parents):-

The name Rohit Sharma would not have existed if these two would not have wanted. They gave him birth which stands at the top and before all the things. Not only this but both of them supported Rohit in whatever his interests was. Despite of knowing that they are not financially capable to fulfil their child's dream, they never said no for anything and that's the quality every parents have. They can never say no to your dreams, doesn't matter how much worse the situation may get. When Rohit was not performing well, his mom used to give him hope and confidence that he will do well and who can refuse the blessing of a mother, even God can't. Whereas his father, having low income, then also he appreciated Rohit to play cricket and now wherever he is and whatever he has achieved is completely due to this two.

2. Ravi Sharma (Uncle):-

He played a major role in preparing Rohit Sharma and his career. The sacrifices that he has went through deserves a stand up charges of applause. Rohit used to live with his uncles at Borivalli and had to travel to Churchgate for practice. He used to wake up by 7 'o' clock and leave at 7.30 around at the morning without eating anything because no food was prepared at the early morning. Then his uncle used to bring tiffin for him later during the practice sessions and matches. He even left his job so that Rohit can get proper guidance and training which was crucial at that point of time. He used to travel with him, sit with him and watch him play and is a huge factor behind Ro-Hit Sharma today. Rohit says about his uncle:-

"My uncle was a big factor in getting me wherever I am. For me, he played a major role and yes, he is a proud 'Cha Cha' now."

3. Dinesh Lad (Coach):-

Whatever you do in your life you need a 'Guru' to guide you and support you. Rohit found him indirectly during an inter school cricket match when he took a couple of Crucial wickets. Dinesh Lad found something glittering in him. Later on he walked to Rohit and insisted to change his school to Swami Vivekananda International School but when Rohit refused it due to financial problems, Dinesh arranged a scholarship for him so Rohit achieved good guidance and skills under him. If that scholarship would not have sanctioned to Rohit, thing would have been quite different. Dinesh Lad completely dominated himself to make Rohit Sharma one of the better cricketers of the world. And it may happen that someday you will be touching the sky through the pillars of success but never forget two persons in your life. First, the one who brought you to witness this beautiful world, your parents. Second, the one who gave the art in your hands to do whatever you want to, your 'Guru'. The pillars by the help of which you are touching the sky don't forget these two have constructed the base for it.

4. MS Dhoni (Leader):-

After the continuous and never ending stories of disappointments, Rohit needed someone to show belief in him and the person can't be better than MSD. The belief that he showed by promoting Rohit as an opener and by giving him the responsibility of his team is doing a immense job for Indian team today as they got the No.1 and the most explosive opener of the world. After that decision, Rohit never looked back.

5. Ritika Sajdeh (Wife):-

No one can stand behind you through whole of your life except your better half. Rohit took 7 most important revolutions of his life with Ritika with the whole world being the witness of their promises. Wherever Rohit played, Ritika supported. In his failures or his success, Ritika was always there to keep her hands on the shoulders to give him that hope which he required at times. At the bad situations too, she kept on motivating him when the whole world left him on his own conditions. That's why she has been Rohit's strength over the years since she started managing him.

Rohit believes, **"I think its the best partnership that I have ever had because whatever I am today is mostly because of her (Ritika). Since I got married, my life has changed completely. Its the best thing that happened to me in so many years."**

14. PRESENT AND FUTURE STAR OF INDIAN CRICKET

In the modern day cricket, not only for India but among all the cricketing nations, its been Virat Kohli who has been a star since a long time now. But in the young Indian team, the player who has been successful in cementing his place in the team since a while after Virat is Rohit Sharma. He has been under shadowed due to the great performances of his captain but if anyone in this Indian team is close to the level set by Virat in terms of legacy, he is Rohit Sharma only. Many cricket experts feel that after some years both Rohit and Virat will find their shoulders at the same height. But I believe its very unfair to compare the two gems of Indian Cricket.

So coming back to the personal aspect. Rohit has done all the hard work and deeds that puts a full stop after the associated word 'star'instead of a question mark. And things are getting better match by match, day by day. Rohit is a star and he will be a star in world cricket because there are quite a few things that only he can do and someone else can't even imagine of doing that. He will try to take this legacy to yet another level through his magical performances.

15. MILLIONS OF FANs

Rohit Sharma have a huge fan following both in the social as well as practical world. The fans are increasing day by day in huge numbers and I am very happy and proud to say that I belong to the same species. And as you all know its a natural process. You go on doing great things by setting examples for others to follow you and they come out in a herd after being inspired. After watching Rohit play, it must have happened that a small kid dreamt of becoming like him just exactly how Rohit saw Sachin and started his journey.

Rohit has around 28.5 million followers socially including all the social media sites he use. 6.4m at instagram, 10m at facebook and 12.1m at twitter which is enough to describe the strength of his fan base. Not only in India but all over the world, the praisers and supporters of Hitman are present. No matter how much he scores or what he do, his fans never curse him instead of that they support him unconditionally. There is a saying that, "If there are fans..

then only there is a star." I believe fans are one of the biggest reasons that motivate a person to do well.

Earlier we only talked about the followers that Rohit himself carries but if we combine all the fan clubs of him and then sum up, it would lead to 55 million followers approx. (all social media sites). Whether its a Twitter handle or FB page or Insta, fans are everywhere to walk along with Rohit's shadow and to follow him. One of them is a fan club titled as "@rohitians_club_45" on Instagram which is one of the biggest fan clubs of Rohit Sharma around social media. There are many more with most of them names as 'Rohitians'. Me too, a huge fan of Rohit sir and these clubs but I don't have any FC because I have dominated my feelings for him on these plane sheets.

Rohit Sharma, you are lucky to have such a fan following all over because the kind of confidence a fan's support can provide, nothing else can't.

16. A GOOD HUMAN BEING

Even if the most successful people of this world doesn't behave in a proper way, they don't get the respect by which they can point their head upwards infront of everyone. So everyone needs to be a good human being first. Our parents, teachers, well wishers, etc they all taught us first try be a good man before anything else. And I can point my head upwards, stare into the eyes and tell with a loud voice that yes!! Yes the one whom I am using my pen's ink is a good human being before the hitman of world cricket and I am so proud of it.

Rohit Sharma have never disappointed his audience through misbehaviour or misconduct. Being such a reputed and star cricketer, he never lets the other person feel that he is talking to such a big personality. Good behaviour, gentle treatment and the quality of helping others is one of the reasons why we all fans consume the drug of love and sweetness, every time we see him doing such good deeds. Let us talk about one of the incidents that took place recently during the SL tour of India 2017. A Sri Lankan fan named Mohammed Nilam came India to support his team. But in the mid way of the series he got the news that his father's health is quite serious and a surgery have to be done so he had to come back home. Nilam did not knew anyone in India and was completely mugged up with the situation. He was not having enough money to book his return tickets. When Sudhir Gautam, a well known fan of team India, came to know about this he asked Rohit for the help and guess what Rohit gave the tickets to Nilam of Colombo along with some money and promised him to meet his father whenever he will visit Sri Lanka. He completed it during the Nidahas Trophy 2018 and went on to meet Nilam and his family also having dinner with them.

Nilam says, **"Rohit called me to the team hotel and gave me the ticket (Rs. 20000 approx.). The surgery**

went well. Rohit has a big heart and when he came to know, he immediately arranged for my return ticket. He is a gem of a person."

This gesture of him proves how good he is as a person. There are many more incidents on social and animal awareness of Rohit Sharma. While visiting the last Northern white African male Rhino, he said sorry on behalf of the whole mankind due to the destruction it had to face. Similarly promoting the world wildlife day and creating animal awareness among people is what make him even better as a human. He requests, **"The rainy season is upon us and I urge everyone out there to open up their building and hearts for the strays out there who need shelter."**

Other than all these activities, he also joins the clean India campaign through his endorsing brand 'Adidas'. He along with the team cleaned up all the plastics and other wastes at Versova beach in Mumbai. Rohit announces, **"TEAM UP TO CLEAN UP!! Join the movement to reduce marine plastic pollution with @adidas. Come out and run for the oceans."**

There are many more stories similar to these all which will never end if I go on telling. Rohit is as simple as you, as me and as all of us. He is not extra ordinary or something like that which many peoples think and Rohit is one of the best person, I know and admire when it comes to humanity.

17. STATS, RECORDS, FAMES AND ACHIEVEMENTS

PART - A

This content comprises of all Rohit Sharma's achievements that he has achieved through his never ending hard work over the years. Since as the name of the book is followed by 2.0, the stats shown are from 2013, the break through year for Rohit. Below are the numbers of Rohit in every match and series he featured.

Note: DNP= Did not played, DNB: Did not bat.

1. ICC CHAMPIONS TROPHY 2013

Date	Match	Score	Venue
6/6/13	IND vs SA	65 (81)	Cardiff
11/6/13	IND vs WI	52 (56)	London
15/6/13	IND vs PAK	18 (32)	Birmingham
20/6/13	IND vs SL (SF)	33 (50)	Cardiff
12/6/13	IND vs ENG (F)	9 (14)	Birmingham
Total:- Mat: 5, Runs: 177, Ave: 35.40, HS: 65			

2. INDIA TOUR OF ZIMBABAWE 2013

Date	Match	Score	Venue
24/7/13	1st ODI	20 (40)	Harare
26/7/13	2nd ODI	1 (07)	Harare
28/7/13	3rd ODI	14 (21)	Harare
1/8/13	4th ODI	64* (90)	Bulawayo

3/8/13	5th ODI	DNP	Bulawayo
Total: Mat: 4, Runs: 99, Ave24.75, HS: 64*			

3. **AUSTRALIA TOUR OF INDIA 2013**

Date	Match	Score	Venue
10/10/13	T20I	8 (8)	Rajkot
13/13/13	1st ODI	42 (47)	Pune
16/10/13	2nd ODI	141* (123)	Jaipur
19/10/13	3rd ODI	11 (22)	Mohali
23/10/13	4th ODI	9* (13)	Ranchi
26/10/13	5th ODI	NR	Cuttack
30/10/13	6th ODI	79 (89)	Nagpur
2/11/13	7th ODI	209 (158)	Bengaluru
Total: Mat: 7, Runs: 491, Ave: 122.75, HS: 209 (PLAYER OF THE SERIES)			

4. **WEST INDIES TOUR OF INDIA 2013**

Date	Match	Score	Venue
6th-10th Nov	1st test	177 (301) DNB	Kolkata
14th-18th Nov	2nd test	111* (127) DNB	Mumbai
Total: Mat/Inn: 2/4, Runs: 288, Ave: 288.00, HS: 177 (PLAYER OF SERIES)			

Date	Match	Score	Venue
21/11/13	1st ODI	72 (81)	Kochi
24/11/13	2nd ODI	12 (19)	Vizag
27/11/13	3rd ODI	4 (14)	Kanpur
Total: Mat: 3, Runs: 88, Ave: 29.33, HS: 72			

5. INDIA TOUR OF SOUTH AFRICA 2013-14

Date	Match	Score	Venue
5/12/13	1st ODI	18 (43)	Johannesburg
8/12/13	2nd ODI	19 (26)	Durban
11/12/13	3rd ODI	NR	Centurion
Total: Mat: 3, Runs: 37, Ave: 18.50, HS: 19			

Date	Match	Score	Venue
18th-22nd Dec	1st test	14 (42) 6 (13)	Johannesburg
26th-30th Dec	2nd test	0 (1) 25 (46)	Durban
Total: Mat/Inn: 2/4, Runs: 45, Ave: 11.25, HS: 25			

6. INDIA TOUR OF NEW ZEALAND 2014

Date	Match	Score	Venue
19/1/14	1st ODI	3 (23)	Napier
22/1/14	2nd ODI	20 (34)	Hamilton
25/1/14	3rd ODI	39 (38)	Auckland

28/1/14	4th ODI	79 (94)	Hamilton
31/1/14	5th ODI	4 (13)	Wellington
Total: Mat: 5, Runs: 145, Ave: 29.00, HS: 79			

Date	Match	Score	Venue
6th-10th Feb	1st test	72 (120) 19 (59)	Auckland
14th-18th Feb	2nd test:-	0 (3) 39* (97)	Wellington
Total: Mat/Inn: 2/4, Runs: 122, Ave: 30.05, HS: 72			

7. ASIA CUP 2014

Date	Match	Score	Venue
26/2/14	IND vs BAN	21 (29)	Fatullah
28/2/14	IND vs SL	13 (28)	Fatullah
2/3/14	IND vs PAK	56 (58)	Mirpur
5/3/14	IND vs AFG	18* (24)	Dhaka
Total: Mat: 4, Runs: 108, Ave: 36.00, HS: 56			

8. ICC WORLD T20 2014

Date	Match	Score	Venue
21/3/14	IND vs PAK	24 (21)	Mirpur
23/3/14	IND vs WI	62* (55)	Mirpur
28/3/14	IND vs BAN	56 (44)	Mirpur

30/3/14	IND vs AUS	5(3)	Mirpur
4/4/14	IND vs SA (SF)	24 (13)	Mirpur
6/4/14	IND vs SL (F)	29 (26)	Mirpur
Total: Mat: 6, Runs: 200, Ave: 40.00, HS: 62*			

9. INDIA TOUR OF ENGLAND 2014

Date	Match	Score	Venue
29th-31th Jul	3rd test	28 (61)	Southampton
In the rest of the tests, he didn't featured.			

Date	Match	Score	Venue
25/8/14	1st ODI	NR	Bristol
27/8/14	2nd ODI	52 (87)	Cardiff
After this game, he was injured and ruled out of the series.			

10. SRI LANKA TOUR OF INDIA 2014

Coming back from an injury, Rohit featured straight away in the 4th ODI without playing any of the three early ones.

Date	Match	Score	Venue
13/11/14	4th ODI	264 (173)	Kolkata
16/11/14	5th ODI	9 (12)	Ranchi

11. INDIA tour of AUSTRALIA 2014-15

Date	Match	Score	Venue
9th-13th Dec	1st test	43 (49) 6 (18)	Adelaide
17th-21th Dec	2nd test	32 (55) 0 (2)	Brisbane
26th-30th Dec	3rd test	DNP	Melbourne
6th-10th Jan	4th test	53 (133) 39 (90)	Sydney
Total: Mat/Inn: 3/6, Runs: 173, Ave: 28.83, HS: 53			

12. CARLTON MID TRI SERIES 2015

Date	Match	Score	Venue
18/1/15	IND vs AUS	138 (139)	Melbourne
Rest of the matches: DNP			

13. ICC WORLD CUP 2015

Date	Match	Score	Venue
15/2/15	IND vs PAK	15 (20)	Adelaide
22/2/15	IND vs SA	0 (6)	Melbourne
28/2/15	IND vs UAE	57* (55)	Perth
6/3/15	IND vs WI	7 (28)	Perth
10/3/15	IND vs IRE	64 (66)	Hamilton
14/3/15	IND vs ZIM	16 (21)	Auckland
19/3/15	IND vs BAN (QF)	137 (126)	Melbourne

26/3/15	IND vs AUS (SF)	34 (48)	Sydney
Total: Mat: 8, Runs: 330 Ave: 47.14, HS: 137			

14. INDIA TOUR OF SRI LANKA 2015

Date	Match	Score	Venue
12th-16th Aug	1st test	9 (24) 4 (16)	Galle
20th-24th Aug	2nd test	79 (132) 34 (55)	Colombo
28th-1st Aug	3rd test	26 (65) 50 (72)	Colombo
Total: Mat/Inn: 3/6, Runs: 202 Ave: 33.66, HS: 79			

15. SOUTH AFRICA TOUR OF INDIA 2015

Date	Match	Score	Venue
2/10/15	1st T20I	106 (66)	Dharamshala
5/10/15	2nd T20I	22 (24)	Cuttack
8/10/15	3rd T20I	NR	Kolkata

Date	Match	Score	Venue
11/10/15	1st ODI	150 (133)	Kanpur
14/10/15	2nd ODI	3 (10)	Indore
18/10/15	3rd ODI	65 (64)	Rajkot
22/10/15	4th ODI	21 (19)	Chennai

25/10/15	5th ODI	16 (20)	Mumbai
Total: Mat: 5, Runs: 255 Ave: 51.00, HS: 150			

Date	Match	Score	Venue
25th-29th Nov	3rd test	2 (28) 23 (39)	Nagpur
3rd-7th Dec	4th test	1 (6) 0 (1)	Delhi

16. INDIA TOUR OF AUSTRALIA 2016

Date	Match	Score	Venue
12/1/16	1st ODI	171* (163)	Perth
15/1/16	2nd ODI	124 (127)	Brisbane
17/1/16	3rd ODI	6 (11)	Melbourne
20/1/16	4th ODI	41 (25)	Canberra
23/1/16	5th ODI	99 (108)	Sydney
Total: Mat: 5, Runs: 441 Ave: 88.20, HS: 171* (PLAYER OF SERIES)			

Date	Match	Score	Venue
26/1/16	1st T20I	31 (20)	Adelaide
29/1/16	2nd T20I	60 (47)	Melbourne
31/1/16	3rd T20I	52 (38)	Sydney
Total: Mat: 3, Runs: 143 Ave: 47.66, HS: 60			

17. ASIA CUP 2016

Date	Match	Score	Venue
24/2/16	IND vs BAN	83 (55)	Dhaka
27/2/16	IND vs PAK	0 (2)	Dhaka
1/3/16	IND vs SL	15 (14)	Dhaka
3/3/16	IND vs UAE	39 (25)	Dhaka
6/3/16	IND vs BAN (F)	1(5)	Dhaka
Total: Mat: 5, Runs: 138, Ave: 27.60, HS: 83			

18. ICC WORLD T20 2016

Date	Match	Score	Venue
15/3/16	IND vs NZ	5 (7)	Nagpur
19/3/16	IND vs PAK	10 (11)	Kolkata
23/3/16	IND vs BAN	18 (26)	Bengaluru
27/3/16	IND vs AUS	12 (17)	Mohali
31/3/16	IND vs WI (SF)	43(31)	Mumbai
Total: Mat: 5, Runs: 88, Ave: 17.60, HS: 43			

19. NEW ZEALAND TOUR OF INDIA 2016

Date	Match	Score	Venue
22th-26th Sep	1st test	35 (66) 68* (93)	Kanpur
30th-4th Oct	2nd test	2 (12) 82 (132)	Kolkata

8th-12th Oct	3rd test	51* (63) DNB	Indore
Total: Mat/Inn: 3/5, Runs: 238, Ave: 79.33, HS: 82			

Date	Match	Score	Venue
16/10/16	1st ODI	14 (16)	Dharamshala
20/10/16	2nd ODI	15 (27)	Delhi
23/10/16	3rd ODI	13 (21)	Mohali
26/10/16	4th ODI	11 (19)	Ranchi
29/10/16	5th ODI	70 (65)	Vizag
Total: Mat: 5, Runs: 123, Ave: 24.60, HS: 70			

20. ICC CHAMPIONS TROPHY 2017

Date	Match	Score	Venue
4/6/17	IND vs PAK	91 (119)	Birmingham
8/6/17	IND vs SL	78 (79)	London
11/6/17	IND vs SA	12 (20)	London
15/6/17	IND vs BAN(SF)	123* (129)	Birmingham
18/6/17	IND vs PAK (F)	0 (3)	London
Total: Mat: 5, Runs: 304, Ave: 76.00, HS: 123*			

Rohit missed the England series in November 2016 which consisted of 5 tests, 3 ODIs and 3 T20I due to injury. Later he couldn't recover and missed the Australian test series too.

21. INDIA TOUR OF SRI LANKA 2017.

Date	Match	Score	Venue
20/8/17	1st ODI	4 (13)	Dambulla
24/8/17	2nd ODI	54 (45)	Pallekele
27/8/17	3rd ODI	124* (145)	Pallekele
31/8/17	4th ODI	104 (88)	Colombo
3/9/17	5th ODI	16(20)	Colombo
Total: Mat: 5, Runs: 302, Ave: 75.50, HS: 124*			

22. AUSTRALIA TOUR OF INDIA 2017

Date	Match	Score	Venue
17/9/17	1st ODI	28 (44)	Chennai
21/9/17	2nd ODI	7 (14)	Kolkata
24/9/17	3rd ODI	71 (62)	Indore
28/9/16	4th ODI	65 (55)	Bengaluru
1/10/17	5th ODI	125 (109)	Nagpur
Total: Mat: 5, Runs: 296, Ave: 59.20, HS: 125			

23. NEW ZEALAND TOUR OF INDIA 2017

Date	Match	Score	Venue
22/10/17	1st ODI	20 (18)	Mumbai
25/10/17	2nd ODI	7 (19)	Pune
29/10/17	3rd ODI	147 (138)	Kanpur

Date	Match	Score	Venue
1/11/17	1st T20I	80 (55)	Delhi
4/11/17	2nd T20I	5 (6)	Rajkot
7/11/17	3rd T20I	8 (9)	Kerala

24. SRI LANKA TOUR OF INDIA 2017

Date	Match	Score	Venue
24th-28th Nov	2nd test	102* (160) DNB	Kolkata
2nd-6th Dec	3rd test	65 (102) 50* (49)	Delhi
Total: Mat/Inn: 2/3, Runs: 217, Ave: 217.00, HS: 102*			

Date	Match	Score	Venue
10/12/17	1st ODI	2 (13)	Dharamshala
13/12/17	2nd ODI	208* (153)	Mohali
17/12/17	3rd ODI	7 (4)	Vizag
Total: Mat: 3, Runs: 217, Ave: 108.50, HS: 208* (PLAYER OF SERIES)			

Date	Match	Score	Venue
20/12/17	1st T20I	17 (13)	Cuttack
22/12/17	2nd T20I	118 (43)	Indore

24/12/17	3rd T20I	27 (20)	Mumbai
Total: Mat: 3, Runs: 152, Ave:50.66, HS: 118			

25. INDIA TOUR OF SOUTH AFRICA 2018

Date	Match	Score	Venue
5th-9th Jan	1st test	11 (59) 10 (30)	Cape Town
13th-17th Jan	2nd test	10 (27) 47 (74)	Centurion

Date	Match	Score	Venue
1/2/18	1st ODI	20 (30)	Durban
4/2/18	2nd ODI	15 (17)	Centurion
7/2/18	3rd ODI	0 (6)	Cape Town
10/2/18	4th ODI	5 (13)	Johannesburg
13/2/18	5th ODI	115 (126)	Port Elizabeth
16/2/14	6th ODI	15 (13)	Centurion
Total: Mat: 6, Runs: 170, Ave: 28.33, HS: 115			

26. NIDAHAS TROPHY 2018

Date	Match	Score	Venue
6/3/18	IND vs SL	0 (4)	Colombo
8/3/18	IND vs BAN	17 (13)	Colombo
12/3/18	IND vs SL	11(7)	Colombo

14/3/18	IND vs BAN	89 (61)	Colombo
18/3/18	IND vs BAN (F)	56 (42)	Colombo

PART - B

Records made by Rohit Sharma in the game of Cricket are as follows. (Excluding IPL): -

- He is the only player to hit three ODI 200's.
- He holds the record of highest individual score in limited over cricket.
- He has hit equal most no of sixes in an innings.
- He has hit the most no of fours in an innings.
- He has made the second highest score on test debut. He is the 3rd Indian to hit centuries in his first two tests.
- He is the only Indian to hit two T20I century.
- He holds the record of highest individual score in T20I by an Indian.
- He has hit equal fastest hundred in T2OI.
- He has scored most number of runs through boundary in a single innings.
- He is the only Indian to hit 100's at Perth and Port Elizabeth.
- He has the highest individual score by a visitor in Australia vs Australia.
- He has hit the most no of sixes in a calendar year and is the only batsman to hit 30+ sixes continuously for five years.
- He has the highest percentage of runs scored by boundaries in an innings.
- He has the highest individual score for India since last 5 years.
- He has hit the most no of sixes and fours in a T20 innings by an Indian.
- He is the only batsman to score a century in all formats of a game in the single tour.

- He was the second highest run scorer of 2017 in ODI cricket.
- He has hit the most no of sixes in T20I for India.
- He has the most no of ducks in T2OI by Indian.
- He has the highest score by an Indian against NZ, SL, BAN, IRE, SA in T2OI.
- He has second most no of 50's in T20I by Indian.
- Only player to involve in 150+ partnerships in T2OI.
- First Asian batsman to hit 300 sixes in T20.
- He has scored most runs in a bilateral series by any player.
- He was the first cricket who was honoured by throwing the ceremonial first pitch for Seattle Mariners in Major League Baseball Club.
- He received the 'Arjuna Award for Cricket' in 2015.

.... And many more

18. CONCLUSIONS AND VERIFICATIONS

The motive of this book as well as mine was to inspire the youth of India and to let them know that struggle, hard work and sacrifice never goes in vain. Rohit's life journey was a perfect example to lead which I personally follow and admire. The book not only will bring you the success of Rohit but also his ups and downs.

While reading the biography, the reader will find that the journey of Rohit is shown in 3 major categories.

1. The struggle and hard work he did to achieve his goal.
2. After reaching the point or achieveing it, its not necessary that you will never be deceived. But the kind of character you enhance will reflect your heat in the comeback.
3. And finally when all the success and fame he gets when his ships full of hard work, determination and efforts comes safely by side and it was now the time to live the life he wanted to.

My motive is to show what ROHIT SHARMA contains behind him because most of the world knows only about the success he has not the process he had to go through. Therefore by this, myself, the author of the book concludes that the book is readable for every age group.

I would like to verify some of my decisions which I took during this mega process.

1. Title followed by 2.0: -

While using your smart phone, you must have observed that there are some versions which are always better than the previous one. Similarly Rohit made his debut in 2007 but till 2013 he was taken into granted many a times but after that a new and updated version of Rohit came up notifying ‘2.0’.

2. The concept of the back design: -

We all know and even many of us believe that ‘behind every successful men, there is a women.’

This was the very reason behind Rohit’s biography there is his woman standing by his side to make it more adorable.

ABOUT THE AUTHOR

'ROHIT-MAN OF MASTERCLASS 2.0'

Written by: Abhinav Lall

The name of the author is Abhinav Lall. He was born on 22th of February 2001 in Rourkela, Odisha. Taking birth in a middle class family where his father is a businessman and mother a housewife, he showed his potentials in this ground very early in his age. He participated in many story writing, essay writing and thoughts expressing competitions and won maximum of them. While studying in class III, he won second prize at school level story writing championship which included students from all class III, IV and V. This sort of performance awared many people about his writing capability. In 2017, at inter school essay writing competition, among various schools of the cities he stood first in that competition. He has also written a short biography on 'wall of Indian Cricket', Rahul Dravid. These several manuscripts produced by him since his childhood determines his interest towards this business. Whenever, he used to get free from his daily routines, he loved to express his thoughts on the blank sheets. It's his own decision to write this biography.

The account details of the author are as follows:-

Instagram: @abhinavlall21

Facebook: @abhinavlall

Twitter: @abhi45

www.ingramcontent.com/pod-product-compliance
Lightning Source LLC
Chambersburg PA
CBHW022158160726
48282CB00024B/247
* 9 7 8 9 3 8 7 8 5 2 4 5 7 *